Hubble & Hattie

The Hubble & Hattie imprint was launched in 2009 and is named in memory of two very special Westie sisters owned by Veloce's proprietors. Since the first book, many more have been added to the list, all with the same underlying objective: to be of real benefit to the species they cover, at the same time promoting compassion, understanding and respect between all animals (including human ones!) All Hubble & Hattie publications offer ethical, high quality content and presentation, plus great value for money.

More books from Hubble & Hattie –

Back cover image courtesy Kerry Jordan

www.hubbleandhattie.com

For post publication news, updates and amendments relating to this book please visit www.hubbleandhattie.com/extras/ HH4931

First published September 2016 by Veloce Publishing Limited, Veloce House, Parkway Farm Business Park, Middle Farm Way, Poundbury, Dorchester, Dorset, DT1 3AR, England. Fax 01305 250479/email info@hubbleandhattie.com/web www.hubbleandhattie.com. ISBN: 978-1-845849-31-3 UPC: 6-36847-04931-7 © Catherine Pickles & Veloce Publishing Ltd 2016. All rights reserved. With the exception of quoting brief passages for the purpose of review, no part of this publication may be recorded, reproduced or transmitted by any means, including photocopying, without the written permission of Veloce Publishing Ltd. Throughout this book logos, model names and designations, etc, have been used for the purposes of identification, illustration and decoration. Such names are the property of the trademark holder as this is not an official publication.

Readers with ideas for books about animals, or animal-related topics, are invited to write to the editorial director of Veloce Publishing at the above address. British Library Cataloguing in Publication Data – A catalogue record for this book is available from the British Library. Typesetting, design and page make-up all by Veloce Publishing Ltd on Apple Mac. Printed in India by Replika Press.

CONTENTS

FOREWORD

I am deeply honoured that Worzel has asked me to write the foreword for this book. As the editor and publisher of monthly magazines about dogs, I often have to speak up for others of his species. It is a great relief to at last have encountered a dog who can write. Let's hope Worzel can give rescue dogs everywhere a voice.

Beverley and Betty.

Betty, one of my three dogs, is almost a Lurcher, She, too, has a great deal to say.

I'll have to whisper this so as not to offend ... but, sadly, unlike Worzel, Betty has only a very limited vocabulary. She is not nearly so erudite as our favourite literary Lurcher.

Betty becomes her most fluent in the presence of important visitors, especially those unused to dogs or, better still, slightly afraid of them. She is aware of manners, but she is also a working dog, and always very keen to get on with the washing up. She tends to stare at guests in a very unnerving way when they are drinking their cup of tea. If she believes anyone is lingering over the last dregs she will quite rudely tell them to hurry up in a most direct fashion.

I have told her many times that she does not need to worry about the cups, that we have a dishwasher, but she obviously feels she does a much better job.

She is the same with socks; she thinks modern detergents simply don't go deep enough, and that they all need a final rinse and a good chew.

Sadly, at almost all other times we are unsure what Betty is saying, but that's never stopped her trying to communicate her thoughts.

She, too, was a rescue so I suspect they all have great stories to tell. If only more dogs could type like Worzel!

I do hope you enjoy this book; If you could read some passages out loud to your own dogs we may find it inspires others to follow in his pawsteps. I hope in time Worzel will be recognised as a trailblazer, and that other clever canines will also begin to put paw to paper.

Maybe, in more enlightened times, there will be a Dog Booker as well as a Man Booker? Worzel's name must be on it, if so.

Beverley Cuddy
Editor of *Dogs Today* magazine
Publisher of *Dogs Monthly* magazine

INTRODUCTION
by Worzel Wooface

Has you ever started a book and, halfway through, discovered that you aren't actual reading the first one in the series? And then frowed it across the room in a paddy? Well, to save you the dents in the wall and your pet famberly members the hupset, I are going to tell you right very now that you need to stop reading this book and go and find the first actual one wot I wrote. Otherwise you will do that frowing fing and get quite actual annoyed.

If you has readed the first one but it was a quite very long time ago, or you're like Mum and can't remember wot you had for tea last night, then here is a bit of a reminder of who everyboddedy is and why they is so weird. And live in our house. I aren't sure if we are weird because we live in this house, or we live here because no other place is weird enough to cope with us all. You'll have to do making up your own mind.

My name is Worzel Wooface and I are a dog and a luffly boykin. As well as being a luffly boykin I are a Lurcher. I have ears that have a mind of their own and eyebrows wot communercate all by their very own. I are a year-and-a-half old and fuge. Sally-the-Vet says I have nearly stopped growing now, which is a good actual fing cos the bed is starting to feel a bit small. It's definitely too small for me *and* Mum and Dad.

I live with five cats. Live is a plite way of describing the daily chaos of wot goes on here. There is rarely a day when one of the cats or me or the hoomans manage to do just living. All of the cats are weird, and it isn't just me that finks this fing. You might assume that cos I are a dog, I *would* fink that the cats are weird, but even the hoomans are confuddled by them. Frank can't control his tail or his happetite, and Gipsy wants to control everyboddedy and everyfing. Mabel sees monsters everywhere and is confuddled by the entire world, and Mouse just confuddles herself: she hasn't got the brains to worry about the rest of the world. Or even the garden.

And then there is Gandhi. Gandhi was borned in this house last year and I has made it my mission to help him avoid being, well, a cat. Being a cat in this house doesn't seem to be a good idea. So I are teaching him how to be a dog. It seems being a dog is the only safe option – even the hoomans are bonkers.

My bestest friend forever is Merlin. He lives just a few doors away from me and he is a Lurcher who forgotted to do growing legs. So, although his birth mum was a long, tall lady Lurcher, his dad must have binned a guinea pig or a Daschund. But apart from being the smallest Lurcher in the whole wide world, he does all the other Lurcher fings wot are himportant, like playing bitey-facey and running and snoozing. Merlin lives with Pip, who is a shrieking, terrier-crossed-with-a-dictator. She is bossy, hopinionated, and In Charge. Of everyone. And everyfing. There is no part of the world that doesn't belong to Pip. Even in front of Dad's confuser, which he forted was sacred territory. It isn't. Pip's just letting him borrow it until she wants it back.

Of all the hoomans in this house, Dad is the most normal and sensible. Dad survives by saying 'yes dear.' All the time. Even in his sleep. He's in love with his boat and sailing. And probababbly Mum some of the time. He also loves me, which wasn't supposed to happen. He was supposed to fall in love with a doggy who was small and convenient and mostly short, not a 26 inch tall Lurcher with legs that do far betterer on land than at sea. But love is a funny fing, so he ended up with me. And Mum.

Mum is one of those peoples who says 'yes' too often. Dad says she is irritatingly helpful and gets involved in all sorts of redickerless fings that he ends up saying 'yes dear' about, and then having to join in. I fink Dad needs to work on the 'yes dear' fing a lot quite harderer, and maybe change it to 'no dear,' but he says he tried that once and fings got very loud. Which was far betterer than the very, very quiet wot happened after that. He says he's not doing it again cos Mum didn't buy any ketchup for a month.

Mum likes doing Panty-Mines and gardening and fostering dogs. Dad mainly likes a quiet life. I are quite very sure he must have realised this after he married Mum, and it must have binned a quite actual shock to him. If he knew he liked a quiet life before he married Mum, he would not have dunned this. Unless it comes back to the 'yes dear' fing again.

There are young hoomans who live here as well. The fuge ginger boyman mostly lives at Universally nowadays. He is learning about science and cider. In that order. At least that's wot he tells Mum. He comes back to visit the sofa and the freezer every so often. And then invites his friends round to scare the cats by singing loud folk songs. If they get too loud, Mum makes them go and sing in the shed, and then they scare all the neighbours as well as the cats.

The previously ginger one is not as fuge or as loud as the fuge ginger boyman. Sometimes, she don't feel quite very well for a long time, and does a lot and a lot of sleeping. Then she stays in her room and it is my himportant work to be gentle and not hupsetting all the cats wot live on her bed. She gets better after a bit but only if she is attached to somefing called the WiFi, and drinks strange, funny-coloured cuppateas.

The young hoomans are nearly not teenagers now, which Mum says might mean she doesn't have to drink so much wine any more. She's tried quite actual hard to be simperfetic and hunderstanding about the hormones and the developing independence and the what-do-you-mean-you're-stuck-in-Norwich-at-4am-and-can't-get-home, but a quite lot less hunderstanding about the tattoos. But she's quite very actual glad that it's nearly over, and she now completely hunderstands why parents spend their kids' inheritance. She's definitely planning on being a batty and eccentric old lady wot runs around the streets in her nightie.

She says she's looking forward to this year. The kids are nearly growed up – one of them has even half-sort-of-quite-very-nearly lefted home – the previously ginger one seems to have discovered the washing machine, and Worzel Wooface is not a puppy-baby boykin any more ∴.

Someboddedy get Mum some wine ... she's gonna need it.

CATHERINE AND WORZEL

Catherine Pickles is a full-time family carer, writer and blogger. Her blog about Worzel reached the final of the UK Blog Awards in 2015.

Worzel Wooface is a Hounds First Sighthound Rescue dog who likes walking, spending time with his family, and chasing crows when given the opportunity. His current hobby is chewing wellies on unmade beds. He lives in Suffolk.

Catherine has fostered numerous sighthounds for Hounds First Sighthound rescue. Her hobbies include sailing, walking, gardening and amateur dramatics, most of which she likes to do with Worzel (apart from gardening, but she doesn't have much choice about it, and the amateur dramatics, which he would hate). She, too, lives in Suffolk, with her husband, two nearly grown up children, and five cats.

DEDICATION

For Charlotte Clark – my local librarian – who does so much more for our community than lend books.

JANUARY

There's somefing outside. Mum keeps opening the front door and muttering that it Looks Like Snow. And then scowling. I don't know wot or who this Snow is hexactly, but I don't fink I'll like him because it's hobvious that Mum hates Snow. Every time Mum opens the door, I consider it my very actual job to nip out and see if I can work out wot she's looking for. But there's quite very nuffink there so all I can do is bring in lots of hevidence of No Snow all over my feet. No Snow hevidence is also known as mud. So now the house is freezing, the floor is covered in mud, and Dad keeps yelling at Mum to shut-the-blinking-door and do somefing useful like make a cuppatea before he goes stark staring bonkers.

The only fings I can find in the garden are the plants I've squashed, and some toys wot I've buried. Oh – and holes. Lots of holes wot I are saving for when I have somefing himportant and smelly to hide. But Mum won't stop opening the front door and wittering on about this Snow. And how it's going to make all the roads icy, and everyboddedy ill, and then no-one will come to the Panty-Mine and all her work for the past four months will have been wasted.

That's wot all the real problem is about, to be actual very honest. This Panty-Mine is all Mum can fink about. She's very in charge of this year's Panty-Mine, and all of Southwold is relying on her to do a good job and raise lots of moneys for Good Causes. Dad would like to do moaning that the house is full of masks and wigs, and the shed is out of action because there's a fuge pretend oak tree that's taking up all the room, and then there's the looks-like-snow-induced-hyperthermia, and there hasn't been anything reliable or hedible for tea since Crispmas. But he can't. Partly because of the Good Causes, but mainly because he made a fuge mistake and forgotted to do Mum a Crispmas stocking, and then wriggled out of it by saying he would be a Supportive Husband about the Panty-Mine and a leading member of Team Mum (Team Mum is in charge of making sure she doesn't have a art attack or hide in the loft stuffing marshmallows in her ears).

I wish he'd done remembering the blinking Crispmas stocking, to be quite very honest. Finding a few pairs of socks and a bottle of bubble bath or a bit of soap would have binned a lot and a lot actual easier than wot's happening now. Cos Dad says if he has to be a Supportive Husband, I've got to be a Supportive Worzel Wooface. Happarently, this means I are not allowed to do peeing up the fuge papermache oak tree in the shed, or do gettering hinjured, or even fink about bogging off on walks. Mum's got a-very-nuff to worry about, Dad says.

The cats have not been asked to be part of Team Mum or Supportive. There is limits, Mum reckons, to how far you can push your luck. They has only one actual job and that is not to get lost or broken or ill. Which is three actual jobs when you do finking about it, but they all comes under the heading of Not Worrying Mum. Gandhi is too busy growing up to be a hunter to worry about Mum or Panty-Mines. His cat mummy was a stray, and she's passed on lots of her surviving jeans to Gandhi – wot he doesn't need a-very-tall cos there's two meals a day and a soft bed and the previously ginger one to cuddle with. Me and Gandhi still do lots of playing when he is indoors, but sometimes when his belly is so full of food he finds it a bit quite very difficult to stay awake. Then I do poking him in the belly and make him burp!

Mouse and Mabel wouldn't be a hasset to any Team. Mouse finds everyfing a bit hard in the brains department. She spends most of her life sitting on the DVD player and forgetting to go outside. Dad reckons Mouse could try a bit harder with the going outside fing, but so long as she doesn't go missing again and cause all sorts of worry and crying, that's going to have to be good enuff. Mabel is too busy being terrified or everyfing and seeing fings to worry about anyboddedy else, unless she's decided that you is today's henemy, and then you is all she can worry about. I seem to be Mabel's henemy of the month, currently.

Frank is too blinking fat and his tail is too long for him to control. He's a great oaf and likely to break all the props and masks so everyfing has to be put in places where he can't decide they look like a soft and squashy, perfickly-made bed for Frank. Cos once Frank's lied on somefing, it won't ever, hever recover.

Gipsy could be a useful Team Mum player cos she's very growed up, and has a way of making everyboddedy do hexactly as they is told. Cos she is very quite scary and has sharp claws wot she is not ever afraid to use. It's a kind of command-and-control with a good-chance-of-death Style of Management. But she was really, wheely poorly sick over Crispmas and Mum says I are not allowed to do anyfing to upset Gipsy cos she is still recovering, and all Gipsy has got to do is get betterer and not cause Mum any worries.

The fuge ginger boyman is hiding at Universally and says he'll come to see the Panty-Mine, but he's never been so glad he passed his Hay Levels in all his life. So, Team Mum is basically me, Dad, and the previously ginger one. I fink we'll be fabumazing at it. Well, at least for a month. I'm sure we can manage it for a month. So long as it doesn't Snow.

January 3

It Snowed. And Mum decided in one of her quite very actual most stoopid moments that I had to go and hexperience it. On my own. Which was not fair a-very-tall because now I has metted Snow, I can see why Mum doesn't like it. It's terribibble stuff, worse than rain! It's cold. It blows about all over the blinking place, and it sticks to every-very-fing. Then it melts and turns into vicious and nasty cold rain wot wriggles between your fur and stings as it snuggles onto your skin. Snow is not nice. And neither is Mum for deciding that I needed to hexperience it. One moment I was quite very comfortable hupside down on her bed, then suddenly I was 'hencouraged' to go outside to get blown about in the wind and the cold. While Mum tooked photos. I was not at all happy about this, and did do coming straight back inside as soon as I could get past the daft woman with her blinking camera.

So anyways ... now I know wot Snow is. And I are not currently very himpressed with it. I are also feeling less like a Supportive Worzel and a very not keen member of Team Mum. I are refusing to go outside and be quick cos there's a rehearsal tonight. I are staying hindoors. Hupstairs. On the bed. I'll go for a wee when it's stopped doing Snow. Even if that means I have to hang on for ... hever.

January 4

Snow is strange. It hangs about on the ground and doesn't disappear like rain. Or turn into puddles which is when I forgive rain for being rain and love it for becoming a puddle. If you do peeing on it, it disappears, and the bits round the edge of where you did pee go yellow. And steam comes off. You can see all the messages wot other dogs have lefted for you without having to sniff them out.

Apart from being a bit blinking chilly on your toes, Snow when it is on the ground is much betterer than Snow when it is flying about. Everyfing is bright and sparkly, and you can see where your feets have binned. We hasn't got a lot of snow but wot we has got is behaving itself and making play time quite actual fun. Apart from when Merlin biffs into a hedge when I is not expecting it. Then all the Snow jumps off the hedge and lands on my head. If I does shaking it off quite very actual quickly it all falls off. If I forget to do this fing, I start to fink I wish I'd let Mum put on my horribibble coat after all, and do shivering, and then Mum says we need to go home before I get too cold. But I hate my coat so I are becoming a master of the spectacular shaky-shaky-jump-jump. Mum can't do shaky-shaky-jump-jump so if she is standing too close to me all the Snow sticks to her instead and she calls me rude names.

****MY FORTS ON SNOW****

❄ Until Snow has decided to stop moving, I does not want to go out in it.

❄ When it is lying on the actual ground it is fabumazing and I want to go and play.

❄ Please wear enuff clothes so that you does not get cold and want to go home.

❄ I are not cold. And me being cold is not the same as you not wearing enough clothes.

❄ I do not want to wear my coat. If you make me wear my coat I will bog off and leave it in the middle of the sugar beet field again.

❄ You are not the first person to tell me not to eat yellow Snow, you is about the seven billionth person.

❄ I are quite very capable of gettering the hard bits of snow out of my toes. All I need is plenty of space on your bed to be able to do this himportant job properly.

❄ I aren't fetching snowballs.

❄ It is never too cold for me to go in puddles.

❄ I can't remember where all the ditches are. Please do reminding me next time; that was a bit of a hactual shock. And not funny.

January 5

The previously ginger one has decided that I has got to have a Noo Near's Revolution. A Noo Near's Revolution is when you start doing somefing or give up doing somefing, and I did get all hopeful that maybe I could do giving up Sit. But she has got other actual ideas.

In our house, the previously ginger one is very In Charge of the cats. Apart from the worming bit and the feeding bit and anyfing that costs money, but that's because she is a teenager and Mum says you can't expect everyfing. But when it comes to making sure the cats is happy and get on with each other and get billions of pictures tooked of them, it's all the previously ginger one's himportant work.

Most of them sleep on her bed, which I fink is a cunning way of keepering me out of her bedroom and hinvestigating all her make-up stuck together with biscuits, but she hinsists it's because it's warm and cosy and she has exerlent cat treats wot I aren't allowed to pinch.

So, it's binned decidered that my Noo Near's Revolution is to Make Friends with Mabel. I fink this is quite very unfair and also himpossible. And I'd rather give up Sit. And Down. And a whole blinking great long list of other hobedience stuff that I aren't that keen on. But happarently giving up that stuff is not a hoption, and that's quite very that.

January 6

I has realised that there is a fuge problem with the Noo Near's Revolution fing. Overnight I did decide that I would actual try my bestest with it all but then I did realise that this Making Friends with Mabel is going to involve Mabel Making Friends with Worzel, which is a bit of a two-way fing wot noboddedy seems to have fort about.

Or hinformed Mabel.

I are wondering how you do make friends with a cat wot hurls herself through the cat-flap before I've got even the black squodgy bit at the very end of my nose into the kitchen, and who refuses to come any further into the house cos I might be actual in there and do Somefing. Noboddedy has ever managed to get any sense out of Mabel about wot the Somefing might be cos she never stays around long enuff to explain.

Dad says he's tried but she's currently hiding in the only bit of the shed that hasn't got a life-sized pretend oak tree in it, wot she is not himpressed about a-very-tall. And she's refusing to come out. Ever.

January 7

Mum's binned explaining more about wot I has to do to be part of Team Mum and a Supportive Worzel Wooface. I fink I has maded a fuge mistake in agreeing to this. My himportant job is going to be staying at home. On my very actual own. Alone. That's difficult stuff for a luffly boykin who's not dunned a lot of staying at Home Alone before.

Mum's binned reading lots about somefing called Seppy-ration Anxiety so she does know all about it, and to make sure she doesn't take anyfing for granted, but she finks she's made a bit of a mistake about it all, really. She says she should have probababbly started this stuff a lot earlier.

Trouble is, Mum's not that keen on shopping trips, and everyboddedy is usually too actual knackered to go out in the evenings. Wot with the previously ginger one being quite often poorly sick, she's rubbish at going out as well. So getting everyboddedy out of the house at the same time, without me, hasn't happened. And it's going to take some horganising to get it to happen now.

We has got a few weeks before I've got to do Home Alone for actual very real, Mum says, so we are going to do lots of practicing until we is all perfick at it.

January 8

Mission Home Alone: Stage One
Mum's had a word about Mission Home Alone with the man who lives next door, and letted him know wot we're practicing, and sorry about the noise if it happens. Fred is a saint, Mum says, for puttering up with being our neighbour. He's also A Bit Deaf which helps, happarently.

Stage One for Mission Home Alone, is that you should not do making a song and dance about going out. Mum hasn't stopped doing song and dance since this Panty-Mine becamed the most himportant fing in the world, apart from me, so I was a bit confuddled by this at first, though that's not quite wot the books very mean, happarently. There's lots of complercated stuff about coming in and out, and leaving for five minutes then coming back, and slipping out of the door without saying goodbye, and Mum's got that bit brilliantly.

Dad says it isn't brilliant, it's cos Mum keeps forgetting stuff, and can't find her car keys, and leaves her purse on the top of the car, and can't remember to shut the door, so she's backwards and forwards like a yo-yo whilst he waits in the car and mutters until she finally finks she's remembered everyfing she needs to take. And then, after five minutes, they have to come back cos they've forgotted the previously ginger one.

I has got to say that by the time Mum has binned in and out seven times and the previously ginger one has binned yelled at to hurry-up-we-haven't-got-all-night and yes-Worzel-does-fink-you-is-a-person-even-if-he-isn't-allowed-in-your-room-so-you-HAVE-to-come, I lose count of who is in and who is out, and it is all quite very hexausting and confuddling, but mainly very actual boring and not nearly as hinteresting as the welly Mum's forgotted to put away.

And I definitely don't want to get in a car with that lot all arguing about how that wasn't hexactly slipping out of the door without making a song and dance about it ...

January 9

This Panty-Mine has even started to hinterfere with my walks now. It's not at all quite very funny. Turns out Mum is playing the Baddy, who is called the Chef of Nottingham, and Louise, Pip and Merlin's Mum, is playing the Goody, Robbing Hood. And they has to do a fight with sticks. Fortunately, they are not bringing the sticks with them on our walks because otherwise I would bog-off big time badly, but they keep doing this strange dance fing wot mainly seems to hinvolve running backwards and forwards and falling over. Then Pip shrieks at them for being stoopid and redickerless, and me and Merlin jump all over them and join in with the wot-you-doing-down-there-have-some-more-mud game. Then they do it all over again. Happarently, me and Merlin aren't helping by jumpering on their heads and joining in a-very-tall. Because that's not wot is going to happen on The Night, so could we please go and do running around and bitey-facey like we usually do because they need to practice? They need their heads examined, if you ask me.

January 10

Do you remember that I got a Noo Near's Revolution quite very actual forced on me? Wot hinvolved Mabel who is hofficially the Maddest Cat in the Whole Very Wide World? She was a perfectly normal cat for a long time but when the previous resident mad cat did go to the Rainbow Bridge, Mabel did take over being mad. It is quite very strange and Mum doesn't hunderstand it. She just gets out of the way very blinking actual fast. It's the honly fing to do.

Mabel is mainly grey with bits of ginger. But she has no grey areas: fings is very black and white with Mabel, and she does making her mind up very, very quite fast. So, you does not get many (any, to be actual honest) second chances with her. If she do decide that she is not happy with you being in the same room as her, she will have a screaming hissy fit, and run out through the cat-flap, or she will get her claws out and do a fabumazing actual himpression of some nasty weapon wot you see in Japanese films. Those wot do make a load of blood and a lot of deaded peoples.

All of this hystericals does make it quite very hard for me to behave like a laidback exerlent Worzel. My favouritist reaction is to scarper. And so would you. But, happarently, this has all Got. To. Change.

Well, I has a cunning plan; Mabel has Got. To. Change first. At least a little bit. A quite lot-a-bit if I has anyfing to say about it. It's actual quite himpossible to ignore a cat wot is whizzing round the room like a balloon that's been pumped up and let go, without showing some kind of reaction. So this whizzing and hystericals has got to stop, and then I will try this redickerless Noo Near's Revolution.

January 11

Mum's dunned somefing hawful to her shoulder. In very fact, that's not quite actual true. I didded somefing to it ... Back in November, one time I gotted quite very over-hexcited to see Merlin, and did my bestest himpression of a racehorse. I did skittering and tugging and prancing, and then a fuge lurchery leap forward. Most of Mum managed to stay attached to her boddedy, when I did this, but her arm came with me. And her shoulder gotted stuck in the middle of a fuge tuggawar. It didn't hurt that much at the time, so she didn't fink that much about it; she was too actual busy calling me a plonker and walking in the hoppisite direction, to make sure I didn't start finking this was how she wanted me to do saying hello-luffly-boykin to Merlin.

At first, it did just do hurting in the morning when she woked up. Now, it's doing hobjectoring at all different strange and random times. She can do her stick-dancing-fall-in-the-mud-fing, but little tiny fings like putting her coat on do hurt her alot. And then she squeals and swears.

Dad says she should go to the Doctor, but Mum says she hasn't got time and she'll deal with it when the Panty-Mine is quite very over.

January 12
I are in the Doghouse, and it is actual very not my fault. Yesterday, Mum and Dad did have fishnchips for their tea wot was a bit of a treat. Gandhi, who is my bestest cat, cos he finks he's a dog, did decide he wanted some of the treat as well, but I did fink it looked a bit strange. He ranned off with some orange and yellow crinkly stuff wot the fish was wrapped in, and began to eat it. Because I are an exerlent hero boykin, I did save him. I did snatch the orange crinkly stuff from him and very quickly gobble it down to stop him being poorly-sick.

I was very quite right about that crinkly stuff, which do taste marvellous on the way down but is a disgusting, yucky, terribibble trick, and not nice at all. It did take me six goes to get the horrid stuff out of my tummy. I did leave it on the carpet, the sofa, and on my bed as a quite very actual warning to Gandhi not to try to eat it again. And just in case Mum and Dad might do forgetting it is horrid for dogs and cats, I did leave lots of it in the middle of their bed as well. I do fink it was my actual dooty to make sure they remembered this himportant fing.

But for some reason I is in the Doghouse, which is all the wrong way round in my head. I did got no brownie points for saving Gandhi, and a lot of rude words about it Serving. Me. Right for being a blinking interfering hogpig. No simperfy. No poor Wooface. No 'you is a hero for saving Gandhi cat from a bad tummy.' Nuffink. Zilch. Nada.

So I is sulking, and on my walk today I did hignore all of Mum's treats and sucked up to Louise instead. She does know I are a luffly hero boykin, even if Mum does actual not.

January 13
The previously ginger one is very just about coping with Panty-Mine, even though it's binned snowing and she's tired and worried about her school stuff. She's helping with the make-up, which I do fink is her perfick job because it is somefing she do take very quite seriously. It takes Mum

about fifteen minutes to be ready to start the day. It takes Dad about six minutes – even less if I do decide to jump all over his goolies to get him out of bed so I can do having the warm patch wot he has specially prepared for me all night. But it do take the previously ginger one about three hours. Just to get ready to go to school. And if her make-up goes actual wrong she shouts and huffs and then has to start all over again.

I have learnt to stay downstairs when the previously ginger one is getting ready. Mum finks this is quite very wise. Not honly is the words that come out of the previously ginger one not suitable for plite comp-knee, the banging and the dropping stuff and the smell is Orrendous. I does not like hairspray or perfume. They do make me sneeze. After the previously ginger one has gonned to school, Mum has to open all the windows just so we can breathe again. And then we do breathe a sigh of relief that she's made it out of the door in time to catch the bus.

January 14

There's binned some hexciting news here today wot I are quite very pleased about. One of the harbour dogs, Lola, did come to visit for the day, because she might be coming to stay for some sleepovers this year when her Mum and Dad have to do going away. Today was a trial to see how I did get on with having another dog in the house, cos it's binned a few months since I did have overnight visitors. I did fink it was all fabumazing and exerlent. I showed Lola the bed, wot she was quite very unsure if she was allowed on, but I did lots of leapering around and did hencourage her so she did know it was okay. When Mum camed upstairs we'd managed to re-arrange the duvet so it was in a big muddly heap, and Lola was all tangled up in the bottom sheet and trying to fight her way out. Mum says we is allowed ON the bed but we is not allowed to change the sheets. Or do pulling the pillows onto the landing. Me and Lola did fink this was a quite very reasonababble request that didn't need nearly so much squeaking or "off now" talk as Mum didded. Once Mum had stopped Lola strangling herself with the bottom sheet, we charged off downstairs to carry on our game on the sofa. Mum says 'scatter cushions' is not a hinstruction, neither.

Lola has two big brothers so she is very used to being with other dogs. Simba and Sam will not be coming to stay when Lola does, and that is the whole very point, happarently. Sam is a good boy but Simba is somefing called a Bad Hinfluence. Lola's Mum and Dad do not fink it is fair to leave Simba and Lola together with other people cos, first of all, Simba would drag Lola off on a rabbit hunt, and then they'd do gettering lost, and then the peoples looking after them would have hystericals. Because their Mum and Dad do know them quite very well, they has gotted fings horganised at home so Simba and Lola cannot do this fing, but hinflicting it on anyboddedy else would not be nice. There is not enuff wine in the world, Mum reckons, to make up for losing someboddedy else's dog.

Lola is a luffly girlkin Dad says. She has quickerly decided she likes our house and our famberly, and mostly does not chase the cats.

She is noisier than me at barking at the neighbours, but that has mostly reminded Mum how quiet and a luffly boykin I are. I do not fink it is a bad fing for Mum to remember how perfick I are at some fings because Lola does 'come.' And 'sit.' And 'wait,' AND 'down,' so I are quite very glad she does barking at anyfing that passes outside our gate. Otherwise she would make me look very bad, and Mum would start that 'sit' fing again ...

So, after Panty-Mine, Lola will be coming to stay with us sometimes, and I are really, wheely looking forward to it. We all is, apart from the previously ginger one. For some reason, Lola has decided that the previously ginger one tastes nice, and keeps giving her a lot of little licks wot is not allowed, especially on the back of her legs when she is half asleep and trying to stagger to the bathroom in the middle of the night. It was honly a few ickle licks, and she really did not have to do screaming the hentire house down cos she forted it was a ghost, or some other actual monster.

January 15

Mission Home Alone: Stage Two
Tonight, everyboddedy in the famberly did actual manage to leave the house and stay left. I has got to say that they seem to be finding this all very much harder than I am. I aren't sure hexactly how long they was goned for but I did a bit of listening to the radio, and founded a Kong wot someboddedy had left lying around on the floor, wot was very quite careless of them I do fink. So that the cats didn't do squabbling over it, I decided I had better give it a good ol' slurpy clean up, and get all the tricky bits out of it, and that tooked some time.

According to our neighbour, A Bit Deaf Saint Fred, I did do some concerned woofing at one point when his takeaway dinner was delivered, but I was mostly quiet and good.

Mainly, I did falling asleep on the sofa, which is where I was when they camed back in.

January 16

Mum did lying down all hunexpectedly tonight. On the kitchen floor. One minute she was standing up buttering toast, then Dad brushed past her and she screamed. Then she clapsed on the floor and made strange crying noises. I aren't sure wot happened next. Mum doing screaming and falling on the floor are not my areas of hexpertise, so I wented and hid on the landing. All I could hear coming from the kitchen were vague whimpers from Mum and a lot of this-is-getting-beyond-a-joke loud words from Dad. Mum is to go to the doctor tomorrow and get somefing done about her shoulder. Or else. Mum said yes-yes-yes a lot, and then staggered up the stairs to check I was still speaking to her, and not too worried about the screaming and the falling over. I was quite very brave, and once Mum had satted still for a bit and I was sure she wasn't going to do yelling or fainting or bumping down the stairs, I gived her a little lick on her chin wot didn't hurted her at all.

Mum's going to go to the doctors tomorrow. She says hignoring Dad's hinstructions is very quite easy most of the time but hignoring me being terrified of her is himpossible.

January 17

The doctor has given Mum some tablets for her shoulder. Fortunately, he does hunderstand about Panty-Mines and pri-orry-tees and I'll-deal-with-it-in-February. To be quite actual truthful, he didn't get a lot of choice. Mum's bossy enuff at the bestest of times but when she is in pain she's hard to hignore.

January 19

Mission Home Alone: Stage 3
Mum and Dad have binned practising the other himportant bit of Worzel Wooface: Home Alone, the bit when they come in after being out. They both has different ways of doing it, but it's working quite very well from my point of view.

Tonight, Mum managed her bestest ever do-not-make-a-fuss-of-Woo when you come home. She walked in, squealed a load of beginning-with-b-words, dropped everyfing and ran out of the door again. Then she spent two hours hunting for the black box full of very himportant fings she'd lefted in the middle of the road outside the theatre, and then forgotted to load into her car. When she appeared quite very later, me and Dad was tucked up in bed, which Mum didn't fink was very Supportive.

Dad says it's very much easier being Supported than being Supportive, and I has got to actual agree with him. It's alright for Mum, Dad says, she can hide backstage when she's not onstage, but he's doing the lighting, so has seen the Panty-Mine done badly, slowly, forgetting-all-the-words a billion times now, and he's got this staring, shell-shocked look on his actual face like he's binned tortured. Which he has – by a bunch of completely terrifying women wearing false moustaches. When he walks in through the door, he has only one fing on his mind: forgetting wot has just happened so he does exerlent determined hignoring of me. He doesn't stop to do anyfing other than flick on the kettle, clapse on his chair, click on Uff-the-Confuser, and furiously look for Boy Fings like Leeds football results or strange lumps of wires for the boat, anything that will wipe out the memory and the scariness of too many women in one room at a time. Heventually, he remembers I is a boy and says hello chap in a hoarse, quite very desperate voice. And then he hears Mum clattering through the back door, dropping stuff everywhere, and quickly jams on his headphones before she starts Talking At Him about everyfing wot happened at rehearsals that night.

As far as I is concerned, nuffink has happened. I've had a lovely, snoozy, wriggly time horganising all the beds, and collecting up shoes and boots, and listening to the radio. I fink I has definitely gotted a better deal than Dad ...

January 21

It's Mum's birfday today but, as always, it's in the middle of Panty-Mine, and she's too very busy with rehearsals to worry about it. She says when you are going to be one or two or eighteen (when you is hofficially a hadult), birfdays are quite very himportant fings. But when you've had hundreds like wot she has, it really doesn't matter; she's got too much else to worry about, so if everyboddedy forgets, that's fine.

Except Dad. Dad is not allowed to forget, and if he does it'll be everyfing that isn't fine and a hawful lot of not speaking to him. A card, a cuppatea in bed, and saying 'Happy Birfday, darling' are himportant, not to mention hessential for Dad getting fed for the next year, and also being able to breathe. You would fink that as this is so very himportant to Dad's survival, Mum would do remindering him, but her birfday is the one fing, she says, that he's got to very remember all by himself.

Fortunately, the previously ginger one, who is mostly a cup-hoarding, Netflix-watching lump hunder the duvet, always remembers Mum's birfday, and can be relied on to do remindering Dad, and sticking notes in his diary, and texting him before he leaves work. And then, every twenty minutes afterwards, to make sure he doesn't get confuddled about why he's standing in the village shop and come home with a sailing magazine cos he started to fink about rudders and other himportant stuff. Stuff that shoves Mum's birfday out of his forts, and then down the back-of-the-sofa bit of his brain cos he's heard Leeds losted again. If we relied on Dad remembering anyboddedy's birfday, the hoomans in this house would all still be six, and I wouldn't heven have a day to celebrate being borned.

So, when there was a card and a cuppatea this morning, and a 'Happy birfday, darling,' closely followed by a smile from Mum and a 'You remembered,' I was quite very surprised. Not about the cuppatea and stuff, but because Mum thinks Dad remembered. But he didn't. The previously ginger one did. And nagged and nagged and remindered and told and sended him back out again. And I are absolutely quite very certain that Mum knows this. Hoomans is strange.

January 24

When Mum has binned all hexhausted from Panty-Mine and clapsed on the sofa, she has been using the time to do some training with Mabel. It do have to be said, though, that Mabel has not completely been an actual willing part-hissy-pant. There has had to be some hinsistering on Mabel sitting quiet and safe on Mum's lap. With Mum's hand holding her quite very firmly. Dad and me has tooked to skulking in the hoffice when this is happening. Dad says Mum is being mean to Mabel, but Mum says Dad is wrong: Mabel can't spend the rest of her life living in the shed where it is cold and dusty. She can, though. As far as I are concerned she can have the whole shed and we'll rename it La Maison de Mabel. Mum keeps shoutering through to the hoffice that 'Mabel is purring' or 'Mabel is asleep,' and that she is definitely making progress. And all the shoutering wakes up Mabel, and she shoots off again. I have decidered not to get in Dad's bad books by telling Mum that he's wearing his headphones, so can't hear a word she's saying ...

January 26

Most of the cats are not at all very bothered about being Home Alone, but Gandhi, although he was quite very okay at first, has decidered he is not himpressed with it, after all. And Frank's decidered to jump on the actual bandwagon as well. They has becomed Keepers of the Kettle. Gandhi likes hooman comp-knee a lot and a lot, and he is very quite actual rubbish at doing hignoring the hoomans when they come back in. When he hears the car coming he bombs through the cat-flap and makes sure he is in the bestest here-I-am, here-I-AMMMM, stroke me now position in the kitchen, which is right next to the kettle. Then he squiggles and wriggles and generally doesn't help with the whole water-filling-tea-bag-sorting-get-out-of-the-way-you-daft-cat stuff that has to happen before anyboddedy can fink about doing anyfing else.

After a bit, someboddedy opens a tin of cat food and gives Gandhi a little bit, cos otherwise he keeps switching the kettle off with his bum, and now Frank has realised that if he sits nearly on top of the kettle and pretends he's binned lonely and needing lots of luffly strokes (which he does not because he's binned asleep on the previously ginger one's bed all evening), he's likely to get an extra dinner. Which he needs like a hole in the head. Dad says trying to get to the kettle at the moment is like trying to prise a mobile phone out of the hands of a 14-year-old girl.

January 27

The previously ginger one is failing badly with Gandhi, and Mum reckons she's going to give him seppy-ration anxiety. As soon as she walks in the door, the previously ginger one tells Gandhi that he's been lonely and missing his mummy, and picks him up and gives him treats. She finks this is fabumazing, and shows how much of a special mummy she is and how much he loves her. Mum reckons she is making Gandhi anxious and teaching him bad habits, and that the previously ginger one should be doing wot Mum is doing with Worzel Wooface, who is gettting this whole Home Alone thing so brilliantly, he didn't even bother to get off the bed and come downstairs when they gotted home last night. Which she is trying not to be hoffended and hinsulted about ...

January 29

Dad's binned permoted! Permoted means he gets to have keys to do locking up the yard, and also do decidering very sometimes wot work other people need to do first. And when John the boss is away, he gets to do Management in the Hoffice. Like wot Lola does. I fink this means he is as himportant and clever as Lola is. But not as clever as Sam cos he can do Management in the Hoffice whilst he is asleep, and without even finking about it. Dad's gonna have to try a very lot harder to reach Sam's level of hexpertise. And he's got to answer the phone, wot Sam is far, far too busy to do.

January 30

We've binned doing this Mission Home Alone every single night for a week now that the Panty-Mine is actual happening, and I has had a-very-nuff. Tomorrow, there is somefing called a Matty-neigh and also a Last Night, which means there is two performances, and two lots of Home Alone in one day, wot I are not pleased about. Mum's not that keen on Matty-Neighs, either, as it's when all the children come to the theatre, and eat sweets and join in the songs and have hystericals when the Baddy scares them. And Mum's the Baddy. Then their Mums and Dads have to watch the Panty-Mine through the little windows in the door of the theatre until the Baddy goes away again. Mum says every time she goes on stage there will be a scurrying mass exit of toddlers. At least there had better be, cos if there aren't, it means she's a rubbish Baddy.

Last Night is dangerous, Mum says. It's when all the famberlies and friends of peoples who are in the Panty-Mine come, and the backstage peoples play all kinds of tricks on the cast, wot is trying to do actoring. Like squirting real water when it's supposed to be pretend, and putting the wrong props on the stage. Fortunately, by the last night, Mum says, everyboddedy knows wot they is doing so well that they can actual do it in their sleep, and none of the audience will care that much if peoples start laughing when they is supposed to be serious.

It's also the last night of Mission Home Alone, wot I do fink it very quite the most himportant fing about the Last Night, cos I are bored now. Very bored. Not lonely or worried or crying ... just bored, and so I has binned finding ways of keepering entertained, and letting Mum know that being bored is not okay for a luffly boykin.

Yesterday, I did eat all the letters that had binned left on the doormat, but everyone was so actual busy that they did not mind that very much. Happarently, it was quite very junky mail so I did fail to be makering an impact. So, today, I did have a scrabble about for somefing that would communercate how bored I is. And I founded some squashy, foamy stuff under the carpet. I did lift up the carpet and have a fine time makering my protest with the foamy stuff. Then I did put the carpet back down again. Everyfing is now a bit uneven at the top of the very actual stairs, and Dad is not that pleased with me.

But I has won! My protest has been quite very actual heard! Today, Pip is coming round to keep me comp-knee! I do like Pip. She is a bit like a babysitter: not naughty but fun, and we will have a very actual hinteresting time talking and playing. Mum and Louise did decide that if Merlin came there might be more chaos than was good for anyboddedy, and I fink they might be quite actual right.

January 31

The Panty-Mine is quite very actual over! Dad says he is never, hever,

hever being a Supportive Husband again. At least not if thirty women wearing false moustaches are involved. Today, he's been listening to loud heavy rock music all day cos he says it's the only way he's going to get the memory of *I will survive* being sung by two pantomime dames out of his head.

But we all did actual survive. Mum is quite very happy and proud about wot she achieved, Dad did exerlent lighting and not worrying too much about his dinner, and the previously ginger one did all of her performances without getting ill or having hystericals.

And I did survive as well. It's a shame about the landing carpet, but Mum says, all fings considered, we has gotted away lightly.

Apart from Frank, he's not light at all. He's fuge after all the extra dinners he's conned out of the previously ginger one.

And he's going on a diet again.

Visit Hubble and Hattie on the web: www.hubbleandhattie.com
www.hubbleandhattie.blogspot.co.uk • Details of all books • Special offers
• Newsletter • New book news

21

FEBRUARY

February 1

Fings were quite very different on my walk today. I did my usual epic running and playing, and I fort fings were going along quite as very usual, but because I can run quite actual fast, before I knewed it I was a long, long, very way away. Usually, I do checking back and staying within yelling distance of Mum, but today, I was having such a fabumazing time chasing pigeons and pretendering to find bunnies that I forgotted all about Mum. Mum says I wented too far. Much too far. And running to keep me in sight and calling my name and doing her T signal – which is wot she does to make herself big and hobvious to me – was quite very hexhausting. And worrying. When she finally persuaded me to remember I had a Mum wot I ought to be playing with, she was super happy to see me, and gived me a treat. Dad says I should remember Mum is quite very good at actoring, and she wasn't as pleased about fings as she did pretend, and I are lucky she didn't do roaring at me. I are glad she didn't do that fing; I don't fink I'd want to come back to someboddedy who did yelling, even if they had just runned half a mile over a ploughed, sticky-mud field, clutching at their bad shoulder so they looked like quasi modo. I did have to go back on my lead after that wot I wasn't that very pleased about, especially as Merlin and Pip did get to do more playing and running about. Cos they is good and do staying near their Mum.

February 3

Dad's quite very not pleased with me. He says I now have 'no recall' and I are somefing called a liability. He wants to know wot Mum has dunned to make me suddenly be all quite very useless at coming back. And Mum's wondering wot Dad's dunned, so fings are actual disagreeababble round here at the moment ...

February 4

It's all about helastic. Wot you can't see cos it doesn't exist, except in Mum's head. Happarently, there is a bit of hinvisible helastic wot runs between me and Mum, and we should both actual hagree about how far that bit of helastic can stretch, and how far I can go before I need to come actual back. Mum says we used to be in tune about that fing. And now, we're not. In very fact, we is so out of tune it's worse than Dad's singing when he's had too much cider. Mum says her helastic is about a hundred metres at the very mostest. Currently, mine is about a billion miles long, and even then the fort of coming back and not finding somefing else to be hintersted in is escaping me. I aren't worried about being on my own or gettering lost, and I should be. I used to be. But now I aren't, and Mum's getting quite actual worried and not enjoying our walks.

I fink I should probababbly be worried too, but I aren't.

Peoples keep saying it's my age, and am I chasing girls? I aren't sure wot I is chasing, or if I is chasing anyfing, but it definitely isn't girls. Or at least I don't fink so. I didn't find any when I was chasing about, just a lot of smelly ditches and a very cross fesant. And neither of them was girls. I'm just having a fabumazing time. Mum says she isn't.

February 5

Mum and Dad haven't dunned going out since the Panty-Mine, and tomorrow will be the first time since it was very over. Dad's binned trying to get out of it all week by saying Worzel Wooface does not want to be Home Alone ever again. But it is all very okay. If they does follow these rules, everyfing will be very quite fine –

****RULES FOR GOING OUT WITHOUT ME****

📋 You is not allowed to leave the house wearing wellies unless I are coming with you. Or your coat.

📋 If you **HAS** to leave the house wearing wellies or a coat, and for some redickerless reason I are not allowed to come with you, you need to put on your wellies where I cannot see you. Or hear you. Ideally, you should actual put your wellies in the shed and change your actual shoes there. Or I will assume you has forgotted somefing himportant. Me.

📋 I don't want to go anywhere if there is a 'dress code' or anyboddedy will be wearing high heels. Dad says he doesn't neither.

📋 You is not allowed to leave the house when there are other dogs outside. Or I will whine and also fink you has forgotten me. Again.

📋 If you touch my lead when you get your handbag off the hook, we is going for a walk. Fink of it like that game Hoppy-Ration. With added mud. Even if you is wearing high heels.

📋 If Dad doesn't know where you put your phone/car keys/purse, it's not likely that I will either, so stop asking.

📋 Please remember to forget to shut the bedroom door.

📋 In very general I do like talking radio stations. But not football. I doesn't understand the rules.

📋 You spended weeks teaching me that you going out is No Big Deal. If I don't come running when you has come back, I are not dead, I are asleep on your bed. And you isn't allowed to feel hoffended. You wanted No Big Deal. Me being asleep on your bed is me doing No Big Deal.

📋 If you has binned out for the evening and there was wine involved, I are probababbly the fing you've just tripped over. Say sorry. Don't just lie there giggling. It's rude.

February 6

Dad really, wheely doesn't want to go to this party tonight, and I aren't helping, happarently. First of all, I has not developed a mystery limp wot would be the perfick hexcuse for him to stay at home with me. And also I went on a bit of an hexplore again today on my walk and I are quite very hexhausted. So, all I want to do is have a bit of peace and quiet and a snore on the big bed. Them going out and letting me get on with this himportant work is very much to my liking.

Dad hates parties. He's rubbish at small talk; there won't be anyfing he likes to eat, he says, and no-one will want to talk about sailing. Worstest of very all, it's with all the scary-ladies-in-tights-and-moustaches from the Panty-Mine.

He doesn't have any quite very actual choice, though. When Mum says Dad has GOT to go somewhere, his choices get quite very limited. Do wot Mum wants. Or else. Which isn't much of a choice. He's really, wheely got to go tonight cos Mum's founded out this year's Panty-Mine has binned nommy-nated for a National Operatic and Dramatic Association award. Getting nommy-nated for an NODA is a very actual big deal, so she's going to drink too much wine and be loud and silly with the other Panty-Mine people. So Dad's decided he's going to have to go, if honly to make sure Mum doesn't come home in a police car. Mum's quite very pleased with him, and says this is why they are so happily married. Just before he stomped off to get in the bath, Dad tolded me that Mum's got that all wrong; it's why *Mum* is so happily married ...

February 7

There do be a new puppy on the block! His name is Nelson, and he is somefing mixed with a French Bulldog. Currently, he's got quite a lot of very actual growing to do before he looks anyfing like his grand name! He lives with Ghost across the road. Ghost is my big, scary friend-if-I-do-behave-nicely. He is a German Shepherd Dog, and quite very actual fuge.

I are not too sure about Ghost. He cannot catch me in a straight line but he is very clever. He can work out which way I might be heading and cuts off corners. When he do catch me, he likes to nip my bum, wot I do find most quite hoffensive and rude. He do mean no harm but it is sometimes a very actual shock. I mean, I is Worzel-Wooface-speedy-boykin, and no other doggy is actual sposed to be catching me. Especially ones that do catch me using their very actual brains.

Ghost is quite actual fond of his little Nelson already, and quite very protective, so I had to use my bestest 'hello-Nelson-please-don't-tell-me-off-Ghost' greeting with him. I did try him out on a bit of racing but he has very short legs, and even when I did go very actual slowly he could not keep up.

When Mum did take a photo of the whole group of us, she did decide that our dog walking gang is a very weird bunch indeed. We has brains and beauty and long legs and short legs, and then there is Pip, who is whoever she do want to be – and I aren't harguing!

February 9

Our friends have goned on their hollibobs, and after the fabumazing time we had in January on our trial run, Lola has come to stay with us.

Last night Mum did make a mistake with Lola's food. She did give her all her day's food in one go, but Lola, she did not do hobjectoring or mentioning this a-very-tall. She did just stuff it all down, and then actual sat asking for more! Mum says this is because she is a hogpig Labrador, which I do fink is quite very rude but actual true.

We was told that Lola is quite very clumsy but she has not broken anyfing yet. She and me did nearly squish Mum and everyboddedy else on our walk, though, because we did not do looking where we are going.

Lola do quite like bitey-facey games. She do lie down, then pounce at me, then do quickly run away and turn round and round in fast circles. Then she do do it again, And again. And again.

Lola is quite actual nice to the cats. I did see her giving Gandhi a nosey-nosey kiss last night, although when Gandhi did first meet her he blew up like a basket ball, and tried to hurl himself through the window. Wot was closed. He did hit the window and then slide down it like wot you see in cartoons. We did not know wot that was all about or whether Gandhi thought Lola was a dragon or something, but he did look very actual quite stoopid and sat and sulked for a bit before getting over it, whilst all the hoomans tried very quite hard not to laugh.

The only fing Lola is struggling with at my house is the cat-flap. You should hear the noise she makes every time she do hear a cat coming in. I are sure she finks we is being robberdobbed or somefink. We are all actual hoping she will realise there is nothing to worry about soon because there are five cats in this house, so a lot of coming and going, especially during the night. I are wondering wot she be going to do when the milkman arrives at 2am in the morning. I are very actual suspecting that she will fink we has been hinvaded by special forces.

February 10

Dad did say that Lola is known to be a bit, well, challenged in the brains department. I fink he means fick. I has never binned convinced about this fing, and now me and Dad do has conflicting hevidence about this.

Last night, mum was a numpty and did forgetting she do have two dogs here. So when we did go out for our after-dinner weesandpoos, Mum did honly let one dog back in. We do all know (and so do everyboddedy in Suffolk, I do fink) that Lola can do barking, especially at cats coming in the actual cat-flap. But it does seem she is not capable of doing 'excuse-me-I-have-actual-been-out-here-for-half-an-hour-on-my-own-and-it's-raining-could-you-actual-let-me-in-you-plonkers' barking. I is very good at this barking, it is a sort of 'I-is-very-hoffended-and-about-to-sulk' woofy kind of yip. Mum always do come running when she do hear it and makes 'Poor Woowoo!' noises, which is all very how it should actual be. So, Mum was in the Doghouse last night because Dad did do telling her off for leaving Lola outside, and Lola did get lots of fuss from Dad, and lots of 'Poor-wetted-cold-Lola' talk. Lola did play along with this fing quite very well, but me and Mum did not fink she was nearly as bothered as Dad did say.

Lola is also very choosy about which house invaders she do not like. And generally gets it completely wrong. Anyboddedy with two legs can stroll in, but if you do have four legs and a meow then you is in trouble. None of us do think this is very actual quite the right way round. But all she do is bark at the cats and she is absolutely flipping fantastic at 'stop' and 'wait' and 'leave it.' I are hoping Mum doesn't notice that she is goody-two-shoes at 'sit.' I have this quite actual horrible feeling Mum will notice soon, though, and we'll be back on that stoopid game again ...

It has taken Lola only two days to work out that dogs is allowed on the bed, especially before the lights go out. And she is quite very exerlent at getting the good bit in the middle. Mum is finking of not telling Lola's Mum and Dad 'bout this because we is pretty sure she is not allowed on beds at home ... we're just hoping no-one do quite tell them or they will start to fink I is a bad hinfluence, and Lola won't be allowed to come and stay again.

February 11

You might remember that I is not food-oriented. Or toy-oriented. Which can make it quite difficult to persuade me to be doing anyfing. But, a few days ago, Mum did take a toy out with us. We've tried this before and it did not go well. Previously, Mum made a right hidiot of herself chucking this thing about and having to pick it up again. I did try to look very actual hinterested in wot she was doing but I must hadmit, I fort she was being a bit, well, weird ...

Anyway, a few days ago on our walk, Mum hurled somefing through the air, and then did let out this fuge yell and turn into Richard the fird, holding her arm and yelling and lurching about. She do say she was in hagony cos of her blinking shoulder wot she fort was getting betterer but hobviously isn't. Anyway, with all this very actual noise and kerfuffle, I thought there might be something worth hinvestigating after all, and founded a yellow ring. So I did pick it up and charge about with it and do shaking it and telling it quite very off for making Mum do that squealing himpression of a wonky king.

Mum was so actual very shocked (to be quite very honest, that is not quite very true: Mum was in so much pain that I coulda started speaking Welsh for all she knew) that she completely forgotted to squeal about Worzel Wooface being a exerlent boykin, and most himportantly, she wasn't at all actual hinterested in any of that confuddling '"bring it here' stuff, so I just gotted to play quite very happily with it on my own.

But TODAY, I did do playing with the toy again, and I did do bringing it back this time so Mum could chuck it again. With her other arm I are pleased to say. Mum says it was worth every single bit of hurting her shoulder. Dad says could Mum just go and see the blinking GP again. Even if he is gorgeous, he'll suffer Mum's gallerping heart and fluttering eyelashes if it means she'll stop clutching her arm and screaming in his ear'ole suddenly. The previously ginger one finks I should proababbly tell you it's her right arm wot is busted, and she isn't having a art attack ...

February 13

The previously ginger one has binned told she's not going to be able to take her exams this summer, and she's really, wheely hupset. Mum's blinking furious. She says she tolded them that the previously ginger one would likely getted unwell at some point, especially if the weather was cold and dark and miserababble, but they didn't listen. And now they are saying she's missed too many lessons being poorly sick and won't be able to catch up. The previously ginger one said she would have binned able to catch up but now she can't see the point of trying to do anyfing, and why she should go to school if she's not going to be able to take her exams? She's going Back. To. Bed. And staying there. Cos she's useless and life is pointless.

There be so many not nice words coming out of Dad's mouth about blinking schools and peoples not listening or doing wot they agreed to do, but mainly wot are we going to do now to keep the previously ginger one going? I has no idea but Gandhi and Frank has gonned upstairs to do exerlent snuggling with the previously ginger one, and that seems to be helping a bit.

February 15

Mabel has begun to get the hidea of this Noo Near Revolution fing. And has quite actual finally started to do her bit. So long as I aren't in the room, and so long as the telly doesn't do any sudden loud laughs or claps, Mabel will sit on Mum's lap. Without Mum having to hold onto her, which only tooked six weeks. I are starting to fink this Noo Near Revolution fing is going to take decades.

February 16

Tonight, Mabel did hachieve mastery of sitting on Mum's lap in the Hoffice. And when I did wandering in, she didn't turn into a screaming banshee. I decided to hignore Mum's franteric hinstructions about Wait and Sit, and Don't Come Too Close! Instead, I did bog off and lie at the top of the landing out of harm's way.

Mabel is still not a completely willing part-hissy-pant in the Noo Near Revolution, and has to be carried from the kitchen to wherever Mum is planning to sit, but Dad says at least Mabel doesn't look like a struggling kid-nappy now. And most of the yowling has stopped. From both of them.

February 17

Mum has binned having lots of phone calls today about somefing to do with Mange. And whether it is the hinfectious type or not. I does not have itchy, scratchy skin so it can't be actual about me. I do not hunderstand why this is so himportant, or why Dad has binned in the shed fiddling about with my old crate and lookering for bits of bed.

February 18

Today, Mabel did sit on Mum's lap without being holded and I did lying on the floor in the same room without getting deaded or losing my eyeballs. It was not wot you'd call a relaxed evening, and I did definitely not do makering eye contact with Mabel. To be quite very honest, I maded myself into the smallest version of me wot I could, curled up, and hoped Mabel wouldn't notice me.

All in all it was a quite actual satisfying evening for Mum, with a lot of Told You Sos, and Dad having to make all the cuppateas cos Mum couldn't possibly move now that Mabel and Worzel were in the same room without the world ending.

I was hoping that me and Mabel could stop all this redickerless Noo Near Revolution stuff now we has dunned Being In The Same Room. And she could go back to living in the shed. But Mum's gotted all over-hexcited and over-hambitious, and has decided there's going to be a Part 2 to this Noo Near Revolution, and that being in the same room is honly half the battle – we've got to learn to henjoy it. Whether we likes it or not.

February 20

Mum says she's not going to walk me off the lead on her own any more. She says I do need lot of reasons to stay closer to her, and currently she isn't a good enuff or hinteresting enuff reason, no matter wot she does. So unless Pip and Merlin come on our walks, I are being stucked on a lead until I has forgotten how to be a blinking hidiot.

February 21

The fuge ginger boyman has comed home for a few days because it's Reading Week at Universally, which is when you catch up on all the fings you hasn't had time to watch on the telly, and get all your washering dunned. And eat for Ingerland! Mum's decided that the fuge ginger boyman has got too skinny whilst he's been at Universally, and he needs fattening up. He keeps telling Mum that he's gotted enuff money and he isn't starving to death, but Mum's been cooking him fuge dinners with loads of meat in them to make sure he's stuffed full when he goes back. Trouble is, the fuge ginger boyman seems to have been surviving on beans-on-toast and hindustrial quantities of porridge, and all the meat has dunned somefing to him. He's all bunged up, and now the chair fing in the bathroom is bunged up as well. Dad finks the fuge ginger boyman will get over it but he's not sure that the plumbering will ever recover.

Whilst he was here, the fuge ginger boyman did hinsistering that the previously ginger one did getting out of bed and coming down the pub with him and his friends. Wot she did do, so the fuge ginger boyman is in everyboddedy's good books, despite wot he's dunned to the plumbering.

february 22

Tomorrow, I has got to go to work with Dad cos Mum's got to go to somewhere called Milton Keynes to collect Somefing Himportant. This is fabumazing news cos I will get to do being a Manager in the Boatyard Office with my great friend, Lola, and her brothers, Simba and Sam. Sam is quite very actual chilled about being in the hoffice, and don't do very much Management because he is too busy snoozing. Simba finks the hoffice is a bit boring and likes to go for a wander around the yard, but me and Lola is always keen and fusey-tastic junior managers, and try quite very hard to make a good actual himpression. We mainly do this fing by knocking bits of paper all over the floor. And woofing every time someboddedy comes into the shop. We do fink it is quite actual himportant that the peoples in the Hoffice do know that someboddedy has comed into the shop, but they say we do not need to do hannouncing it, and believe it or not, they already know cos they is taller than us and can see over the shelves!

Me and Lola do not fink this is good enuff, and peoples need to be woofed and barked at so that they do have the hoption of coming to say hello-luffly-boykin-and-girlkin before they do buy the strange lumps of metal they need to stop their sail falling down, or their bottle of gas. We fink we is an added actual bonus to the customer's overall shopping hexperience. Happarently, we just need to shut up before we drive everyboddedy nuts.

It's alright for Simba ... when he sees someboddedy he likes, or if it looks like someboddedy has forgotted to shut the shop door, he just waits until he isn't being watched and hops over the gate to the hoffice. And goes for a stroll into the sheds, and is quite very exerlent at hanging around and not bogging off. Me and Lola can't work out how to get over the gate so we have to do barking and woofling to get some actual attention and fuss.

february 23

When Mum gotted back from collecting the himportant fing from Milton Keynes last night, it was a very ickle smelly surprise. I has got a new foster sister, but she is not like my last foster sister, Pandy, a-very-tall. You should remember Pandy. She did wot you would call making a Lasting Himpression all over our house. Like breaking the stairs and generally being ignormous and squishy and healthy. But the ickle new foster sister is none of those fings.

She is quite actual thin, and her skin is all sore and she has baldy patches. She has no hair on her tail, and her muzzle is crusty. All of her eyelashes seem to have binned eated away as well. Her back end is almost completely bald, and her tail looks like she borrowed it from a poorly rat. All-in-very-all, she looks more like a Muntjac deer than a dog. She is also hincredibly, hunbelievably smelly. Well, you would smell, too, if you was covered in poo.

On the way home from Milton Keynes she did do poos inside the crate actual four times. The first time Mum did stop to clear it up but after that she did actual decide just to drive back with the windows open or they would never get home, and the only fing that was going to stop the poo was not being in the car. And not being scared. Mum says Milton Keynes feels like it is the other side of the moon, and so would you if you had to drive that far with a doggy and that much poo.

When she did arrive here Dad did lift the crate and the doggy and all the poo out of the car. Mum did phone to warn him 'bout this needing to be actual done, and he didn't run away down the harbour, which I fink was quite very actual fabumazing. Then the poor doggy did have to go straight into the bath to wash off the poo, but she couldn't have a luffly soak or nuffink cos of her very poorly sick skin wot is sore with that Mange fing Mum was talking about on the phone.

None of this was wot you might call actual hideal. Wot shoulda happened is that my new foster sister should have comed straight into the house and goned in her luffly snuggly crate, and had a blanket putted over it and be very carefully hignored until she had gotted used to the new smells and sounds. And then tooked out every forty minutes for a wee in the garden, and then goned back in the crate and carried on being hignored ... As you can quite actual tell, Mum and Dad has dunned this before. Lots of times.

But because of the poo and the sore skin and being wet and chilly from the bath, she hadded to sit in front of the fire and get warm and dry. She did this bit quite actual perfickly.

Then she did meet me. And she did do a poo, even though I did my most gentlest, bestest waggy tail, hello-does-you-want-to-play-wow-you-do-still-smell-terribibble, which she did not hunderstand. She did fink I was scary so then I did fink she was scary. It was a bit like in those films when two scaredy peoples do meet, and they both scream and run away. We did do that. After that, I did decide hiding upstairs on the bed was the most sensibibble fing to do and stayed out of the very actual way.

The cats do not care for sensibibble courses of action. Or poos. Or scaredy doggies. They has set out their actual stall, as hoomans do say. The doggy has decidered she is going to be cat-safe and cat-trainable which I do fink was a very actual wise move. Frank, Gispy and Mouse do NOT be taking any nonsense off any doggy. Gandhi do fink he is a dog anyway so he do not care. Only Mabel has taken to her shed, but then Mabel will take to her shed given any hexcuse so that isn't actual surprising, and the Noo Near Revolution fing has had to be putted on hold for now.

Since then, there has been quite a few more poos but no wees indoors. In very actual fact, when the doggy do be taken outside for wees, she do do an exerlent good-girl-be-quick. Mum do not fink there is a prolem with house-training, so she do be mainly hignoring the accidents and trying not to make a drama out of the crisis cos that would make things actual worse. And probababbly mean more poo.

Currently, noboddedy has even fort about finking up a name for my new foster sister – apart from Poo Pants but that's not one she can take out into the world, Mum says, so we will fink about finding a betterer one once the new doggy has settled in. And stopped pooing every five minutes.

february 24

Today, fings have goned very quite much betterer. Last night, Poo Pants did sleeping in her crate all night without any fuss at all. At least, there was no fuss once Mum did work out wot all the yelling and shoutering was about. At first, Mum did fink Poo Pants was hobjecting to being in the crate and wanted to come out which was Not. A. Hoption.

There is five cats in our famberly who need to be able to wander about. And house-training to sort out, but more very himportantly of all, having a safe place to call their own is the first very most himportant fing frightened and poorly-sick doggies need to have. Once they do feel safe, they can start learning other stuff and become happy. Mum wondered if she was going to have to do sleeping beside the crate to help Poo Pants settle, but it turns out that Poo Pants very liked her crate, it's just that her blankies weren't arranged as she did want them. So she yelled at Mum until she came to sort them out. It tooked a bit of working out but it seems Poo Pants is very quite par-ti-cool-ar about her blankies. And very quite par-coo-li-ar as well. Weird, to be actual honest. Turns out Poo Pants likes her blankies completely all over her head with just her nose sticking out. Then Poo Pants did this funny, muttery noise and felled completely, zonkingly asleep.

Mum reckons Poo Pants is going to be a right little character. Going from pooing all the way home in the car to horganising hoomans to straighten her blankets in six hours flat is quite actual himpressive. She's now being called Princess Poo Pants.

Best of very all, at seven o'clock this morning, there was lots of yelling and demanding noises coming from the crate, wot I can tell you was all about lemme-out-I-need-a-wee. Seven o'clock and out for a wee is very quite acceptababble, and user-friendly, Mum says. And definitely much betterer than the constant stream of poo we had yesterday. The crate was clean this morning as well, so fings is quite actual lookering up!

february 25

The previously ginger one is in lurve with Princess Poo Pants, even though she do still smell Orrendous because of her poorly skin. And Princess Poo Pants has decided that the previously ginger one is her favouritist hooman, so they is both in a happy, stinky love-fest. The smell is being very actual put up with and hignored because she is cute and ickle and delicate and cuddly. And dorable. Unlike Worzel Wooface who is a fuge oaf and a daft plonker. Princess Poo Pants can curl into the teeniest, tiny little ball and does settling down all comfy next to the previously ginger one. And doesn't do wriggling about and sticking her feet up the previously ginger one's nose. Basically, Poo Pants is currently behaving like a cat which is why she's pop-poolar with the previously ginger one.

It's all very okay, though, cos Worzel Wooface is getting lots of attention from Dad, fanking you kindly for asking. Dad's just glad it's not him that's the Chosen One for Princess Poo Pants because she still stinks, even if she is cute.

Princess Poo Pants is still a little bit actual unsure of me. There aren't any more poos happening but she is pretendering that I don't hexist, and does not want to play. She just wants to hide under a blanket on the sofa with the previously ginger one. Mum says it's early days, and she really isn't in any fit state for bitey-facey or playing at the moment, so I are allowed to say hello and have a bit of a sniff, but I aren't allowed to do anyfing else.

February 26

The previously ginger one has decided that Princess Poo Pants is going to be called Hazel. Mainly cos she's stopped doing the endless poo fing but also because Poo Pants isn't wot you'd call a recommendation. Hazel has binned chosen cos she's little and brown and curls into a tiny, tight little ball like a nut, and it's a nice name without being too complercated or posh or grand. Hazel is still very odd looking with all her baldy patches and no eyelashes, so a nice simple name is wot she needs. A posh name might be too actual much for her. And make her poo ...

February 27

Hazel might be a very nice name without being too complercated, but it seems that no-one can remember to call her that, and she has spended all day being called Princess-Poo-I-mean-Hazel.

February 28

Mum says the next person wot forgets that Hazel is called Hazel is making the cuppateas for the rest of the day.

Everyboddedy is remembering quite actual well now ...

MARCH

March 1

Hazel went to see Sally-the-Vet today. She had to have some skin scrapes tooked. Do you know, she did just put up with it. She is very, very quite big and tough and ... really, she is none of those actual fings. I fink she's just living up to her name and is nuts. I would have very actual had to be given sleepy meds and trauma ferapy, but Hazel did just have it done with no fuss or bother. Mum fort this was quite very sad, really. She says that cos Hazel has had lots of terribibble fings happen to her she just accepts more terribibble fings happening again. I fink this is quite actual hawful.

How-very-ever, we do fink Hazel is going to recover quite actual well. Even though she is not called Princess Poo Pants any more, she has holded on to the Princess bit quite very well. She's learnt that going outside in the cold and the dark is actual not much fun, and refuses to walk on the gravel, so she is getting a lot and a lot of picking up and plonking down. She's also gotted all the hoomans learning to hunderstand Hazel-speak quite actual well so they all run around making sure she is warm and comfy. I'm sure she's got some Whippet in her.

March 2

Hazel and me has been doing playing today. And she is starting to look like a doggy rather than a Muntjac deer! Her hair has begunned to grow back on her tail so she doesn't look like the back-end-of-a-rat, and her face is definitely not all crusty. Dad says she is turning into a Pretty Little Girl.

March 3

Yesterday, we did take Hazel out to show her the sights. And to see wot she was like in the big wide world, and whether she did do coming actual back. We is quite very lucky where we do live cos it is safe, and there are places where you do have to work quite blinking hard to bog off, so even if you do has the recall of a banana you is not going to get into trouble.

Hazel wasn't interested in bogging off a-very-tall. She did love to do run and chase with me, but she was not as fast as me. This was quite actual himportant cos I do not know wot I will do if I hever meet a doggy who is faster than me.

Mum does fink that Hazel is badly out of condition, and she very likely IS going to be as fast as me once she has got a bit fitter, and she might even be faster! I do find this very actual quite hard to believe.

She do not be liking to go into puddles, though, and when I did splash past her she did look most actual hoffended.

Hazel do like to pootle about with the hoomans bestest of all. She does lots of lookering to see wot they are doing and likes to suck up for treats. Hazel would do anyfing for a treat, and I has had to tell her off a couple of times for trying to take mine out of my quite very actual mouth!

The only fing that Hazel did see that might encourage her to do bogging off was a seagull, but I can tell her now, it is pointless. I has tried to catch billions of birds, but they do this flying away fing that makes it actual himpossible to catch them. And if the bird does not do flying away, then you is in real fuge trouble cos that means it will be an actual Swan or a Goose, and everyboddedy does know they *eats* dogs.

March 5

There comes a time in every actual foster doggy's life when they do realise that they is safe and warm, and are not going to get beated up or chucked out. And then you do start to see wot the doggy is actual like. It's a bit like when you get a noo girlfriend and you do careful remembering to wear matching socks and brush your hair. And then, after a while, you can relax and start cutting your toenails in front of the telly.

Well, over the past couple of days, Hazel has dunned starting to relax, and – oh boy – do we have a fuge problem on our very actual hands and paws.

Today, Hazel managed to get all four of her feets onto Mum's dinner plate at the same time. Whilst it was balanced on Mum's lap. And then she managed to get her head onto the plate long enough to eat Mum's pork chop. One minute Mum was lookering at the telly, wondering if the golfman was going to get the ball in the hole, and the next minute she had a side order of Hazel with her dinner. Or to be actual very truthful, *without* her dinner cos Hazel wolfed most of it in two seconds flat. By the time Mum had realised wot had happened, the chop was gone and Hazel was tucking into the mashed pertato.

Mum leapt up, the plate felled on the floor, and instead of dinner Mum had a flipping sticky mess of cabbagey gravy to clear up.

And a very quite hupset Worzel who does not like hunexpected bangs and dramas. Or words beginning-with-B.

Dad's gone to the shed to find more stairgates cos that will Not. Be. Happening. Again.

March 6

The good news is that Hazel hasn't worked out how to jump over the stairgate to get to Mum's dinner. But she can scream for blinking Ingerland. Wot I do find very quite disturbing and distressing. So I did rush up to the gate and do telling her off. Then I got hejected from the sitting room cos Mum says she doesn't want me getting any stoopid ideas about guarding. So I went upstairs and sulked very actual big time.

Hazel carried on screaming and yelling so she had to go in her crate. And then she carried on screaming and shoutering and being quite very Orrendously loud from there.

The previously ginger one tooked her dinner to her bedroom to eat, and Dad's finking of taking his dinner to the car. And I are going too.

March 7

Hazel is not starving. Hazel is having three meals a day of a fabumazing raw diet, and getting training treats of dried liver and little fishies and cheese. The fuge ginger boyman went into the kitchen tonight and discovered that Hazel had decided to add dead teabags to her diet. From the pot on the kitchen work surface, wot was the honly fing apart from the kettle she could have eated. He reckons there must have binned at least seven thousand dead teabags in there, given the mess he had to clear up after she'd opened them all and scattered them everywhere. Mum isn't sure wot's more concerning: Hazel finking dead teabags are worth eating or the fuge ginger boyman cleaning up a mess he didn't make.

Dad's trying to be hunderstanding. Tonight, he did say that cos she was a stray and didn't ever have enuff to eat for ages and ages, Hazel's got it into her head that she has to eat everyfing she sees or smells, just in case she never gets another meal again.

March 8

Tonight there is going to be a cunning plan, and no dinner for Mum. Or at least not proper, normal, everyboddedy-in-front-of-the-telly dinner. Instead, there are going to be a blanket on the floor of the sitting room and some toast for Mum, and a hawful lot of 'off,' 'no, leave it' for Hazel. And NO food from the hoomans' plates, and even more himportantly, no Hazel on the hoomans' plates. Especially that bit. Removing Hazel from the room is not actual working so she's going to have to learn that she doesn't own every bit of food in the house.

I has to say it did go betterer than I hexpected. Hazel was much easier to do teaching and hexplaining to when Mum wasn't trying to juggle a plate of wobbly spaghetti bog-nog, and the toast was hinteresting enough to count as food but controllababble by Mum. It's going to take a few days, but Mum says she's not going to have to eat her dinner in the bath after-very-all.

March 10

Mum did shoutering a lot of rude words at a man today. For nicking her car parking space. Usually, Mum is very growed up and keeps her forts about stoopid peoples inside the car, but she's hadded no sleep for days, and is trying to juggle a food-pinching Hazel, a Worzel who is hignoring her, the previously ginger one who has gotted really, wheely unwell again, and a shoulder wot is either not moving or making her scream.

I are quite very pleased that I has gotted all this Home Alone stuff sorted, so I wasn't actual there to see Mum having hystericals. The previously ginger one was, though. She says it was mortifying and hembarrassing (and quite very actual fabumazing but I'm not allowed to tell Mum that bit, cos otherwise she'll start worrying she's teaching the previously ginger one bad manners on top of everyfing else).

Worzel Wooface

March 11

Dear Hazel

Candles is not food. I fort you should know this fing.

From your luffly boykin

Worzel Wooface

Pee Ess - And neither are the hyacinth bulbs wot you digged up in the garden wot are poisonous, and now we has to go to see Sally-the-Vet. And I has got to go, too, cos Mum is worried that I did eat some as well. Which I did not cos I are not hobsessed - or stoopid.

March 12

Apart from bin-raiding and food-scavenging (wot she could win medals for), Hazel do seem to be quite very user-friendly. She is learning her noo name really actual well. She has no strops, or snaps at peoples, or grumps or grumbles. She does be HATING gravel, and going into the garden where it is cold, but suffers being plonked out, especially if I do go with her. She is getting better at the weesandpoos fing as well, and today, not only did she have a go at playing with me, she also did doing playing with the football!

March 13

We did finally get a bit of sun today, and both me and Hazel do very agree it has to be worshipped. We do this fing by dragging all the blankets and beds and spare jumpers wot peoples have lefted around to the perfect spot, and get Mum to open the front door. She might be freezing cold cos it's March, but we really, wheely need that bit of sunshine wot we don't get unless the door is open. Hazel did exerlent muttering at Mum that this is wot we needed her to do. She's quite very useful like that. Mum putted on an extra actual jumper to suffer the March cold, but we was happy cos we had SUN!

March 14

As part of Hazel's edercation, I did introduce her to Pip and Merlin, all proper-like. They has been saying hello-pleased-to-meet-you through the gate for the last couple of days, but today we did go out for a run and playtime together.

Hazel did not do letting me down or hembarrassing me in from of my friends a-very-tall. She do have fabumazing doggy manners when introduced all proper-like, and did have a very quite exerlent play with me and Merlin.

Pip did not do any telling her off cos she didn't actual need to. We was all quite very himpressed cos usually Pip do have to tell new doggies how the world do work, and that she is actual always In Charge, but Hazel was respectful straight away.

Instead of Pip telling Hazel the rules of the actual game, she did spend her hentire walk telling Mum and Louise everyfing she had to say.

I DO NOT LIKE THIS HOUSE TODAY

Somefing fell off the wall today
And landed with a fump
I do not like the walls today
They blinking made me jump

Mum says it was a picture
Wot crashed down on the floor
She says I shouldn't blame the wall
It was a slamming door

I aren't allowed to blame the door
Mum says that isn't fair
A hooman left it open
To let in some fresh air

I do not like the walls or doors
Or pictures or fresh air
Or curtains rustling in the wind
They're giving me a scare

That picture could've landed
On my flipping 'ead
I do not like this house today
I are going back to bed.

On and on she did go, and drive both the hoomans bonkers-crazy with her endless chatter. I won't be telling you wot the hoomans did say to Pip in the end cos it was quite actual rude and not fit for plite comp-knee.

March 16

The doctor has sented Mum for somefing called fizzy-oh-ferapy. From wot Mum said today, fizzy-oh-ferapy hinvolves talking, a lot of words beginning with B, and hexplaining that you is losing the will to live. When Mum said the losing-the-will-to-live fing to the fizzy-oh-ferapy man, he hadded a right panic and sended Mum back to the doctor for a hemergency hinjection, and please could Mum unsay that stuff about losing the will to live cos otherwise he's gonna have a fuge load of paperwork to do? And phone Mental Health services. Mum unsaid it. There's nothing wrong in her head that won't get betterer if her blinking shoulder would Just. Stop. Hurting.

March 18

Mum's hadded the hinjection wot seems to have worked a little bit. And the fizzy-oh-ferapy man knows wot is wrong with it as well. And how to fix it. Mum fort about kissing him when he said this but that didn't seem like a actual good idea, so she did crying all over the poor man instead. She hasn't stopped talking about him all evening. He's quite very young and actual good-looking. And has a beard. Dad says he doesn't care if he's Brad Pitt: HE'LL kiss the blinking man if he fixes Mum's shoulder.

Fizzy-oh-ferapy isn't about talking. It's about being squashed. Almost satted on. I has no idea a-very-tall why this is working but happarently it is. Mum's got exercises to do at home, and Dad is doing lots of helping her. Today, she managed to move her arm a ickle teeny bit without fainting. She did go very pale, though ...

March 19

Hazel was quite very actual skilled and himpressive last night. She did achieve mastery in getting on the previously ginger one's bed. In general, I do not be going on this bed, mainly cos it is always full of cats wot can be a bit actual possessive about it. I do find that there is easier and less spiky, hissy-fitting places to have a actual snooze, but Hazel was keen, and sometimes you do have to let folks find fings out for their actual selves.

The first time she did get on the bed, Mouse did do telling her to bog off with claws. But Hazel is determined, AND more oppymistic than me so we did have a chat and I did give her some advices. For the benefits of other doggies, this is my actual advices about Getting On A Bed With A Cat Already On It (fanking you kindly for putting up with this not-very-snappy title).

First, choose your cat. Gandhi is easy-peasy. He do fink he's a dog so you can be practicing this stuff with him as much as you like, but do not be finking that if you can get on a bed with Gandhi on it, you can get on a bed with any ol' cat. Cos you actual can't. Gandhi is fabumazing, but he is not an actual proper cat.

Mabel don't go on beds, she only ever goes hunder them so don't never, ever, HEVER go hunder beds. Ever. And if Gipsy is on a bed ... walk away, slowly. It is only ever going to end at the vets.

So, that do leave Mouse and Frank. They is wot you might call reasonababble cats in that there is a reasonababble chance you will survive if you do hencounter them.

If you do be wanting to get on a bed with a proper cat already on it, you must not be doing eye contact. You has to be getting on without lookering at the cat, and also without very standing on it. You has to saunter all casual-but-determined towards the bed, and then jump on neatly and GENtly. GENtly is very himportant cos if you do wobble or bounce the bed, the cats do stop being cats and become Lerts. Lert cats are not your friend. You must not be showing any kind of weakness at this point, cos if they do see any doubt in your boddedy then they do hissy-fit-ninja-hellfire-hexplosions.

Once you has gotted onto the bed and not done bouncing it and not done turning the cats into Lerts, you need to lie down quickerly and GENtly. That GENtly fing again. And do not be doing too much turning round and round and round and ROUND in circles trying to get all your legs in order, cos that will hinvolve turning your back on them too many times, and they might do gettering hideas.

Once you is lying down on the bed, you has wonned the game of Owning The Bed. The cats will either stalk off in a quite actual sulk, or will hignore your fabumazing victory and pretend it has very not happened. And go back to sleep.

Hazel did try out my advices with Mouse and fings did turn out betterer than I fort. She did heven manage to hachieve touching bodies with Mouse, which I do have to actual admit I has not ever, hever binned able to do. Being very quite honest, I do not fink it is actual worth the risk, but Hazel is at that stage of life where you has to try stuff just for the very heck of it.

I are currently trying to tell Hazel that attempering the double-cat-manhoover with both Mouse AND Frank is called Pushing Your Luck, but she is all cocky now after last night. Frank is generally less likely to become a Lert but he is built like a badger. If he do wake up or she do stand on him then things will end quite actual badly. Hazel don't want to listen to that bit of advice, though. She's determined to actual try.

March 20

The spirit of Easter and the Easter Bunny seem actual very lost on Gandhi. Every day this week he's broughted Mum a present and dumped it where it can't be missed. Unless you are carrying a basket of washing down the stairs and can't see your actual feet. And slip on it and nearly break your neck. Mum says Easter. Is. Cancelled.

March 21

My Hazel loves the sun. It is her bestest fing hever. Apart from food but that is some bonkers haddiction wot isn't good for her, so noboddedy finks that's to be hencouraged or smiled about. But she is fabumazingly silly about the sun and she do follow it wherever it goes ... even up the stairs. As the sun moves, so does Hazel, until she is balanced badly on about three different steps. Then she falls asleep. And slides all the way to the bottom with a fump.

March 22

Hazel has definitely gotted too many actual bits of Whippet in her. Today, she did decide that she would like to be wearing pee-jim-jams. She is not a whole actual Whippet, she is a Lurcher, and I do fink she is badly letting the side down. And also giving Mum ideas about whether I would like peejamas. I do not want peejamas ... hespecially not lime green ones wot glow in the dark. Hazel looks redickerless and also quite actual scary. And I will not be playing with her when she is wearing them. Hazel finks she looks wonder-very-ful, and did strutting, and muttering and chatting about them all evening.

March 23

Mum says the fact that Hazel has just gone outside without being asked, told or plonked is hevidence that miracles do actual happen.

I still cannot be persuading Hazel to put her feets in the puddles, though. She do fink getting her toesies wet is disgustering, and do look like a Orrified cat if she do think she might be gettering wet.

March 24

We've dunned it! Tonight, Hazel did lie down on her bed without screaming or shouting or trying to get onto anyboddedy's dinner plate. And there was no 'leave it' or 'off' or nuffink. In the same room as everyboddedy. When they were eating proper dinners. She did lying down like a good girl, and was quite actual relaxed about it all. Dad says *that's* stretching fings a bit very far cos she was watching everyfing the whole blinking time, and if anyboddedy had dropped somefing they shouldn't have then she woulda binned there like a shot, but she did lying down being good.

Mum says she's has been snapped at, runned away from, pooed on and hignored. She's had dogs who won't use the stairs or who try to eat the cats. She's had one who finks a lead is torture, and ones who won't stay in the garden, and ones who guard their safe spaces and their toys. But she has never, ever, hever had a foster doggy who was as difficult to deal with as Hazel and food.

It's binned hexausting, and there has been a few hysterical phone calls to Hounds First, but tonight, we fink we might have quite very actual cracked it!

March 25

It must be that actual time of year. Today, Hazel didded somefing that I did almost hexactly a year ago. Hazel founded the look-out post in the garden wot all the hoomans call the garden table. Noboddedy ever uses it as a table for eating, mainly cos it's always stuffed with plants, but it is perfick for hobserving the world outside the garden. And it's also a quite very sunny spot as well. All-in-all it is the perfick spot for watching the world go by.

Hazel was quick to get onto the table, but then she did have a panic that she had dunned a wrong fing. And she did look all sad and worried to start off with. Mum did tell her that this are the HONLY table she is actual allowed to get on, and was a bit hoping that Hazel could tell the actual difference between an outside table and a hinside table, cos she's spended the last week persuading her not to get on the table in the kitchen. In the end, she fort there was enuff differences for Hazel not to get actual confuddled ... and anyway, she looked quite actual sweet and dorable perched on the garden table. Sometimes, sweet and dorable wins over everyfing. Even when you is a foster mum trying to help a foster dog be ready for a forever famberly.

Gettering onto the table was no problem for Hazel, but when it camed to gettering off, she did have some troubles. For a very actual start, the table is surrounded by gravel wot she finds prickly and shifty and cold. So leaping off was not a hoption. And she also had to do working out how to do wriggling round plant pots, and using the bench as a step down, and where to put her back legs whilst she was worrying about where her front legs would go. It was all a bit of a disaster, in quite actual fact. Her ears went all flappery, and I fort she was going to try to use them to fly off the table like that elliefant in the films, but in the end Mum did take pity on her and gave her a lift down. Otherwise she would still be stucked on the table wriggling about and muttering to herself.

March 27
Hazel is soon going to be ready for a forever famberly. I do fink it actual very HIMPORTANT that she is dopped by someboddedy fabumazing.

She says she do want a home where they do lots of treats. And there is a carpet to practice sitting on cos she has made it stonkingly clear that no carpet, no 'sit.'

She also wants someboddedy who will tuck her in with a blanket at night, but she aren't fussed if there's no bedtime story.

Mum and Hounds First are on the hunt for the perfick home for Hazel now. One with very high cupboards and bins with padlocks. And no bulbs in the garden ...

March 29
****HIMPORTANT DISCOVERY****
It is a quite very well known fact that Hazel will eat HANYTHING. Candles, old teabags – everyfing is food to Hazel.

Except squid. Not even if you actual pay her.

Therefore, squid cannot be a food. I do not know why you actual hoomans eat it, cos if Hazel won't touch it, you probababbly very actual quite shouldn't either.

You did hear this first from Worzel Wooface ...

March 30
The fuge ginger boyman has managed to get himself into somefing called the London Philharmonic Choir. I find this very hard to believe. I didn't

even know he could sing. I mean, I've hearded him howling in the bath, and singing with his mad friends when they has dunned drinking too much wine, and they get out their guitars and pretend they is the next best fing to Pink Floyd, but happarently, he can quite very proper sing. Well, he's managed to convince the peoples at the London Philharmonic Choir he can, anyway.

Mum says it is a true actual fact that the fuge ginger boyman can sing, and she's quite very glad he's actual doing somefing with his singing, and making all the monies she did spend on him being a chorister when he was an ickle fuge ginger boyman worthwhile. I are really struggling with this but Dad says it is all true. The fuge ginger boyman used to be one of those cute and dorable boykins wot you see on the front of Christmas cards. And sing carols. And – according to Dad – be quite actual naughty and tough as old boots, and full of energy to the point of very hexhaustion for all the peoples who look after them. Choristers aren't cute. Which is a good actual job, cos the fuge ginger boyman is many fings, like messy and loud and forgetful, but cute he aren't, and I can't himagine a time when he ever was! Happarently, he is going to be singing in lots of himportant concerts, and somefing called the Proms. Mum just hopes he remembers to brush his hair.

March 31
****FABUMAZING NEWS****

I are delighted to hannounce that Hazel wented visiting on Saturday, and she has founded her forever famberly.

She is being dopped by some peoples who are both actual quite clever, which is a quite good fing cos Hazel is a very actual smarty-pants-brain-box-doggy, who do be needing peoples who can keep up with her.

Hazel did do luffly cuddling and saying hello-hinteresting-people, and she did like them quite very much! Hazel was actual herself on the visit, and did do peeing on the carpet, and went on a food hunt, so her new Mum and Dad do know that she is still a work-in-progress. She did say hello-nicely to the cats, and the cats did do telling Hazel that they is in actual charge.

She is going to be living quite near to me, so I are hoping we will be doing catching up in the future.

Hazel won't be going to her forever home for a few weeks cos her new famberly has got a hollibob booked, so she will be staying with us for a bit longerer. Which means I has got a bit more time to do making sure that Hazel has all her Sighthound skills in place ...

APRIL

April 2

I has got a hinjury on the side of me. It is my first proper actual Sighthound war wound. It isn't deep or bad, it is just one of those scrapes wot Sighthounds do get from trying to play bitey-facey at the speed most cars travel. It is hinevitababble, Mum says.

Mum's attempts at hinspecting my scrape have goned the same very actual way, as usual ... I do fink she shoulda learned by now that any trying to do nursing me will result in me hiding in a dark place where there is not enough light to SEE anyfing, and most himportantly of very all, DO anyfing.

It's my war wound and I has got it all under very control, fanking oo very much.

April 3

I have just broughted terribibble shame on my famberly.

We wented for walk and I did see a fesant. There is nuffink I do like more than a fesant for chasing. I has never caughted one but I do love it when they do rubbish flying and epic squawking.

Hanyway, I did see a fesant and off I belted. Hazel was goody-two-shoes and did come-and-get-a-treat and don't-you-dare-follow-Worzel. But I was very off!

Then in-hex-icker-babbly I did find myself in a strange garden. It was one of those gardens where getting in was quite very easy but working out how to get out again was very much harderer. After the fesant had dunned bogging off and Mum and Dad and Hazel were trying to catch up with me, and I was wondering how I had gotted into the garden and why I couldn't blinking get out again, I did see that there was a pond. The gettering out of the garden became very less himportant than jumping in the pond. Which I did do. Chasing fesants is hot and tiring work and a cool down seemed like a fabumazing idea.

And that's where I was when Mum and Dad caughted up with me. Lollopering around with the goldfish and the tadpoles and having a very actual fabumazing time. They couldn't work out how to get into the garden so Mum did her usual flapping and demanding Dad DO somefing. Quietly. There was a hawful lot of hissing and wondering if the peoples in the house were in and if I'd killed all the fish with my lummoxing about. Heventually, I did decide that I'd hadded a-very-nuff and Dad managed to find a hole in the fence to crawl through and get my lead on and do crawling back through the hole, dragging a very soggy but hextremely happy Worzel Wooface.

Mum says I are not allowed to be hextremely happy. I should be mortified like wot she is.

April 4

After yesterday's hadventures and hembarrassments, it seems that Mum and Dad are now in hagreement that the Time Has Come. And so is Sally-the-Vet. I might still be a bit very quite anxious and worried about some fings, but this hindependent Lurcher who don't need no Mum has got very actual to the point where it could be dangerous. And hexpensive and hembarrasssing.

Mum's hadded a chat with Hounds First and they is quite very pleased that the Time Has Come. Because of my terribibble start in life and because Sally-the-Vet did advising it, and also because I wouldn't stop growing, they were happy to wait a bit longerer than is usual but it is all very hessential and part of being dopped.

I has no hidea a-very-tall wot they is going on about to be truthful but they seem to have stopped wailing about the pond fing and me being a blinking nightmare and wondering if I can ever safely be letted off my lead again, so I fink this Time Has Come stuff is probababbly a good fing.

So, once Hazel has lefted for her forever home, everyboddedy has promised me that fings at home are going to be quiet and settled and horganised so that all my finking is calm and I are as actual relaxed and chillied out as I can be. Then, when the Time Has Come actual comes, everyfing will be very quite okay.

April 5

Today I was hinvited to go and see where Hazel is going to be living when she is dopped. I can say I do very actual approve and did proper checkering out the place for Hazel. Hazel was far too busy gettering cuddles and having her photo tooked to be able to do this all properly, and so I fort it was my job to make sure the himportant stuff was all horganised.

In the garden there was no pond but there was this big tank wot is supposed to be a bog garden. Everyfing in the tank was very quite black and sticky and gooey. I did have a very quite exerlent dig about in it to get rid of all the plants so it is ready for when Hazel moves in, and when she finally decides that getting her feet wet is a quite very good fing.

There is all kinds of different walks around where Hazel will live with lots of safe places to play and run around. Mum has gived Hazel's new famberly lots of advices about Hazel and her food fetish, and they is all hexcited and very actual ready for the arrival of Hazel next week. Who isn't going to be called Hazel anymore but Hattie, which I do fink is very quite sweet and dorable and a little bit cheeky which is just wot Hazel is.

April 6

Mum's very fussy about forever homes. She says she has to be, otherwise we'd do keeping every doggy wot has ever comed here as a foster. You cannot do teaching a dog and making it happy and discovering its favourite fings and then just forget about them once they has goned. And letting them go in the firstest place is very much easier when you know that their life is probababbly going to be betterer even than the one they have with you.

Hattie-Hazel will be a honly dog, which we do all fink is a quite very good idea, with her food fetish, because if somefing has binned eated, then they will know it has binned eated by Hattie-Hazel. And won't be dragging all the other famberly dogs down to the vet on the off chance they has been as stoopid or redickerless as Hattie-Hazel. I can tell you for nuffink that it isn't a hexperience I would want to wish on any other actual doggy. Hattie-Hazel needs to keep her redickerlessness to her actual very self!

April 8

Tomorrow, Hattie-Hazel is being collected to go to her forever home. Mum's binned wearing the same t-shirt in bed for the past week, and I has to tell you it has gotted pretty whiffy. It's going to go with Hattie-Hazel to her forever home. In a sealed bag with lots of sorry-about-the-smell words. I has been jumpering all over Mum in bed whilst she's binned wearing this t-shirt so the smell of me can go with Hattie-Hazel as well. I do not want her to be forgetting me neither. Mum says it isn't so we don't get forgetted, it's so Hattie-Hazel can have somefing wot smells safe and familiar in her new home. Finking about it, when Hattie-Hazel did arrive here and there was no safe smells for her, she did blinking loads of her own stinky, smelly poos, wot was horrendous. So even though the t-shirt is a bit actual disgustering and very quite mucky from when I gotted a bit over-hexcited doing rubbing Worzel smells all over it, and not remembering about the cuppatea-you-daft-oaf, it's got to be betterer than Hattie-Hazel's previous attempts at making somewhere smell like home.

April 9

My work is done! Hazel is being picked up in an hour and I will miss her very muchly.

She has a very actual luffly new home, and if she follows my hinstructions to the letter she will be sleeping on the bed and making sure everyfing is how she likes it within 48 hours.

To selly-brate I has dunned writing a poem for the mostest hilarious, food-thieving, duvet-diving mutter monster my famberly has ever metted. Wot is a hawful lot of words to avoid saying mostly Whippet I do fink. Pee Ess – it's on the next page ...

April 11

Mum's stucked in the bath and Dad's in the Doghouse, and I are a luffly boykin who has somehow gotted to be telling Dad that he needs to take his blinking headphones off and rescue Mum before she freezes to death. Cos she can't get out of the bath with her poorly shoulder, and Dad promised to help her, but he's forgotted and is playing a game on Uff and can't hear Mum yelling.

I are not that clever. I are more decorative than useful in very

HAZEL-HATTIE

Hazel-Hattie, Pudding and Pie
She'll eat the lot and then she'll try
To steal your breakfast, munch your lunch
Pinch your tea and crunch your lunch

Hazel-Hattie, sweet and kind
Likes her blankies, you will find
Over her head and tucked in tight
Do it right, she'll sleep all night

Hazel-Hattie, good as gold
On her walks if it's not too cold
If it is, she will not leave
Her bed unless you haul and heave

Hazel-Hattie, do be gentle
With the cats or they'll go mental
Remember, cats have teeth and claws
They is in charge; they is the laws

Hazel-Hattie, happy and bright
Do not cry too much tonight
Remember everyfing you've learned
This perfick home is one you've earned.

general, or a belting-around-chasing-crows type of doggy. Acting as a go-between a furious, freezing Mum and a deaf, dense Dad is quite very actual not one of my talents.

I fink Mum's gotted me muddled up with one of Gran-the-Dog-Hexpert's dogs. Gran-the-Dog-Hexpert doesn't have normal dogs. They don't do lying around being comfy, they do hobedience and hagility, and most actual Orrendous and worrying of all, somefing called Working Trials. Heven the Cavalier King Charles Spaniels – wot in most famberlys can rely on having a cushy life being lazy companions – do it. And they like it! Seriously! They fink it is all fabumazing fun. Gran-the-Dog-Hexpert gets very actual over-hexcited about Cavaliers being working dogs who are quite very capababble, and not just for looking cute.

I look cute. Everyboddedy says so, which, as far as I is actual concerned, is good enuff. I very actual quite definitely don't want Gran-the-Dog-Hexpert giving Mum hideas about how capable I could be.

Currently, I are refusing to go in the bathroom, which Mum finks is cos I usually avoid going in there in case someboddedy has the stoopid idea that I smell. And decide to Do Somefing about it. It's not that; I just don't want anyboddedy joining dots about me going in the bathroom, and Dad remembering that he needs to rescue Mum, and finking I had anyfing to do with reminding him of this actual fact.

Cos that might make Mum fink I are more capable than I want to be. And that would be heven worse than her freezing to death.

April 12

Dad remembered about rescuing Mum before she did dying or divorcing him, although she says it was a close actual fing and sometimes Dad is a Fortless Pig. I fink they has comed to a hunderstanding now after Mum did Not Speaking To Dad for the rest of the evening, and then threatening to forget to pay the broadband bill, like he forgot to rescue Mum.

I fink this could all work out very well for me. Dad's currently trying quite actual hard to be more capable and less of a fortless pig, and Mum's still sulking a teeny bit. I are doing careful and considerate being with Mum, and having all the kisses and strokes that would normally be going Dad's way. Wot he can't have cos he's too actual busy being capable and cooking dinner. Mum seems to have forgotted her stoopid hidea about me rescuing her from the bath, and is very quite satisfied that I are cute and keeping her comp-knee on the sofa, whilst she do decide whether Dad has dunned learning his lesson.

April 13

Dear Gypsy-the-Foster-Fridge

Fank oo for sending me pictures of wot you do look like nowadays. We used to fink you was fuge when you was here before you got dopped by your forever famberly. But that is very nuffink to wot you is like now. You aren't really the size of a fridge any actual more; you is more bungalow-shaped. I do fink.

Yesterday, we did get a actual message from your forever Dad who said he is tearing his hair out cos you has turned into somefing called a Diva. Mum says a Diva is a stroppy lady who wants her own way. Dad says she sounds like a typical woman, but Mum tolded him off and stomped up the stairs in a huff.

Your Dad says you is being stroppy-diva-Gypsy cos you is having a season, and you has turned from a sweet, cuddly girlkin into a growling, howling monster, and the boy dogs in your famberly are very quite confuddled and hupset. But they does not be wanting to do making babies with you, cos a) they is not completely bonkers, and b) they can't. I is very quite glad you is far away in Lincolnshire being a Diva cos I don't fink I would like it very much neither.

Mum did have lots of simperfy for your Dad and your Mum. She says I are going through the 'terribibble twos' as actual well, and being hawful at coming back and not going on my lead, and finking I are allowed to do wotever I do want out on a walk. It's all quite very hexhausting for her, but fank goodness I has finally stopped growing so that soon the Time Will Come when she can Do Somefing About It. I do not know wot this somefing is, but happarently the same somefing is going to be happening to you, as actual well. Then, hopefully, fings will be calmer and you won't keep turning into a Diva, and I might fink coming back is a good idea again.

I does hope you is feeling betterer soon, and you don't eat your brothers.

Lots of love

From your luffly boykin

Worzel Wooface

Pee Ess - if you do find out wot this somefing is, please do be telling me.

April 14

I've just hadded the worstest actual news ever. Hever. Pip and Merlin are moving. Not far. In actual very fact, just to the next village. But the next village isn't three doors away. Three doors away means you can look out the door and realise it's a fabumazing day, and decide not to waste it doing hoovering. And be out on a walk in twenty actual seconds.

Or if Mum or Louise has hadded a rubbish day and need to do talking loudly-and-very-fast-a-lot-but-not-cross, and without anyboddedy else hearing, they can stand in the middle of a field yelling and kicking stones for Pip, whilst me and Merlin do running around and squishing each other, until they has gotted all their words out and feel betterer.

But now we is going to have to be horganised and do car travelling, and it's not going to be the same.

Life has just done changing. For the worstest, worstest ... WORST!

April 15

If yesterday was my worstest day ever, today has binned one of Mum's bestest days ever. Wot I don't fink is very quite fair. Life shouldn't do all this uppy-downy stuff. It's very quite confuddling and makes everyfing in the house all noisy and very not settled.

Mum's Panty-Mine honly went and wonned! Getting nommy-nated was a quite very actual big deal, but quite very actual winning is unbelievababble! They has fishally gotted a NODA, which is fabumazing and like winning a Noscar in the amateur dramatics world.

Mum's quite actual shocked; she's never dunned producing and directing a Panty-Mine before.

Dad's hoping she'll choose to end her career on a high note, and never, hever do it again.

April 16

Today, Mum gotted a letter saying she has to go and get her foot wot hexploded last year on the Three Peaks Fing actual looked at to see if it can be fixed. Mum's still getting her shoulder squashed in fizzy-oh-ferapy, and it's all working quite very well, but she doesn't fink she can cope with being squashed in the shoulder department, *and* bended in the foot department at the same time. Dad says she doesn't have any actual blinking choice, and if she turns down the foot-bending she'll end up at the back of the queue again.

April 18

As part of the keeping everyfing simple and relaxed with no bogging off or hystericals about chasing fings and getting losted or stucked, since Hattie-Hazel was dopped I has maded a new friend, whether I actual like it or not. Her name is Lindy and she is a Staffordshire Bull Terrier.

You remember when you was a small hooman, and you hadded to be friends with the person who had the cricket set, or the football, well, I has to be friends with Lindy because she has a fuge garden wot is enclosed by a six-foot fence all the way round. Wot Mum says is currently hessential ...

Mum says Staffies sometimes get called rude names. I fink this is daft. I has only ever metted two Staffies, so I can't be saying I has wot you would call fuge hexperience, but both of them has binned luffly. And quite very helpful.

The first one I met was Edith. I metted her when I did very first come to live in Suffolk when fings were quite actual new. Mum wanted to do somefing called a Hassessment on me, to find out the fings I was okay about and also any fings that I needed to learn. My Mum called Edith's mum cos Edith is the safest, mostest bomb-proof doggy Mum has ever metted. And her Mum is also very actual hexperienced at dog training, and could do giving Mum lots of advices and suggestions. Edith is perfick if you do have a doggy wot might need to learn some manners, or if you want to see wot happens when you let a doggy off their lead for the first time.

Everyboddedy needs an actual Edith in their life. She is very steady, and does exerlent hignoring of bad behaviour, but doesn't get scared or react. She's like a fabumazing bestest auntie; you can tell her all your secrets and disasters and she won't do fainting or telling your mum. But because of wot Edith looks like (basically hexactly like a Staffordshire Bull Terrier, cos that's wot she is), peoples do assume she is not going to be any of those fings. It's all quite very stoopid and wrong.

So, when Mum said I was going to meet a new Staffie friend called Lindy, I was actual quite pleased and hexcited. Lindy is a bit like Edith but older. And fatter! And a bit bonkers-crazy if you do ask me. Lindy lives with Mostyn, who is Gandhi's brother. Now, you does know that I fink Gandhi is my own actual cat, and he does fink he is a Lurcher cos I did teaching him that fing. Well, Mostyn was dopped by Lindy in a quite very different way. Lindy did decide that Mostyn was her baby, and did cuddling and trying to feed Mostyn from her own boddedy. Mostyn tooked very fuge hadvantage of this and did suckling from Lindy. Now he finks Lindy is his quite very actual Mum. It's all quite very strange, and not wot peoples fink Staffies should be like a-very-tall. So, just like Gandhi finks he is a Lurcher, Mostyn finks he is a Staffie. And peoples fink Staffies are mean or gressive ... Peoples, in my hopinion is quite actual weird ...

Mum says I are going to be gettering lots of visits to Lindy's garden over the next week so I can have playtimes and do running around like a mad fing without getting hurted or lost, because I are not going off-lead in the big wide world again for a little while ...

I still hasn't worked out wot is going to be happening but Mum has started on about this Time Has Come again. Dad says he doesn't want to talk about it, and keeps on changing the quite very actual subject ...

April 19

The fuge ginger boyman is being really, wheely weird. He keeps phoning Mum and asking complercated questions about electrickery bills, and should he have a water-meeter? Growed-up stuff. In June he is going to be moving out of his room in college, and living with friends in a house. On Their Own. Without A Mum. Somehow, he's ended up being put in charge of making sure the bills are going to be paid and horganising everyfing.

To be quite very actual honest, the honly fing the fuge ginger boyman used to be able to horganise was making a mess in the kitchen, and losing his wallet whilst eating seventeen egg sandwiches, and forgetting to get his hair cut. Stuff like that; quite very actual unhelpful but impressive multi-tasking. Mum keeps wondering out loud why he's in charge of all this paperwork and how come he's binned nommy-nated as the most responsibabble. Dad reckons the other peoples must be a right shambles if they reckon the fuge ginger boyman is the most capababble, but the fuge ginger boyman says they is all history students, as if that explains everyfing.

The previously ginger one is already asking if she can go down and stay at the fuge ginger boyman's new house in June. Dad says she just wants to meet the fuge ginger boyman's housemates cos there aren't any boys lefted in Suffolk she hasn't dumped or declared childish. And if she wants to go to London in June, it might be a good idea if she started getting out of bed in Suffolk, wot she has binned not managing to do again. Mum says this isn't quite actual helpful or tactful but I fink Dad's got a point.

April 20

Dear Gandhi

The previously ginger one wants me to tell you that she doesn't want your dead baby bunny, especially not at half-past six in the morning. And definitely not in her actual bed. She's not doing speaking to you anymore, which is why I has binned asked to pass on this very himporant actual message.

From your luffly boykin

Worzel Wooface.

Pee-Ess - I'll have it.

April 21

Tomorrow the Time Has Come. Mum says we all has to be exerlent luffly good hexamples and that it is very nuffink to be actual worried about.

The Time Has Come, I has now founded out, is to do with removing two out of the three parts that make up my gentleman bits. I are going to be lighter in the trouser department, and my brain will do going back into my head again, hopefully.

I are trying hard to do believing Mum about this nuffink to worry about fing, but she keeps needing hugs, and talking-tos from the previously ginger one about not worrying, and yes, Worzel will wake up, and yes, Sally-the-Vet knows he's a Sighthound, and all about the annersfetic fing.

Dad's being useless. He keeps flinching and saying poor Wooface. Mum has told him to stop being so hidiotic so he's goned down to the harbour to fiddle with bits of his boat, and so he can't be a bad hinfluence. And also not do finking about wot is going to happen to Worzel Wooface and imagine it happening to him. Mainly that last bit, if we is completely actual honest.

This morning I did do my bestest to help Dad get over these forts. And when he woked up I maded sure I was lying on top of him with my soon-to-be-goned gentleman bits six inches from his actual nose. Now he's feeling quite positive about it all, and pleased that this is the last time he's going to see THEM first fing every blinking morning.

April 22

I are back safe and well from my hoperation. I are not having to wear a buster collar because I are an actual good boykin who is leaving everyfing a-very-lone.

Apart from feeling sleepy and being spoilted rotten, I are feeling just the same as I did yesterday. But I are enjoying the special attention and gentle strokes very actual a lot and a lot.

April 23

Dad is in the actual Doghouse. He do keep teasing me. He says there did used to be a man singer called Danny La Rue, who Mum says did dress up like a lady. Dad has started to call me Worzel La Woo instead of Worzel Wooface because of my hoperation yesterday.

I do not know hexactly why he is finding this so actual blinking funny. I do usually have a quite exerlent sense of humour, but I is sore today, and still quite actual sleepy, and feeling a bit actual sensitive about everyfing, so I is not himpressed. A-very-tall.

April 24

Mum's going away overnight. She's gotted to wear high heels and a dress. Me and Dad have both quite very actual opted out of the hoccasion. We're rubbish at high heels and dresses.

So Dad is actual in charge of me and my after-hoperation care, and he says we're having chips for tea! He whispered this to me like it was a himportant secret hannouncement, but we always have chips for tea when Mum's away. We just don't do telling her ...

April 25

The previously ginger one did getting out of bed today. This shouldn't be news but, hunfortunately, it is. She did actual come downstairs and do talking to people and watching the telly with Dad. It's the quite very first time I've seen her for a week, so I did my very actual bestest hello, and very careful not leapering all over her on the sofa.

April 26

This morning I has been to see Sally-the-Vet about my hoperation.

Yesterday, when Mum was doing stuff in high heels, fings did do a bit of actual swelling up, and Dad was a bit quite actual concerned. As Mum was off wearing high heels, Dad was in charge, but Google did tell Dad that everyfing was okay, and that everyfing was very normal, and it wasn't very nuffink to do with all the chips I had eated. He very wisely and actual quite bravely did decide that he would not do telling Mum about the swelling in case she gotted a taxi all the way from London to Suffolk, and did make him quite actual bankrupt.

Although the swelling in that department has started to get a bit smaller, Mum did fink a quick check-up was a good hidea. I've binned given some more painkillers, but Sally-the-Vet did agree with Dad that everyfing is actual fine. Dad is quite actual relieved about this fing because he is not allowed to break Worzel Wooface unless he is prepared to face the hell-in-seven-shades-of-purple that would be Mum if anyfing happened to me when he is In Charge.

Mum would like to be a bit more growed up about the fort of somefing happening to me. She tried it once for about a minute but it didn't work, so now Dad knows that she do be going to have hystericals if she do heven fink there might be somefing the matter.

Tomorrow I are allowed to go for walk on a lead, which will also help make the swelling go down. I aren't sure how my feet moving will make the swelling go down on bits that don't do walking, but I are quite actual pleased about this because I are getting a bit bored, and Mum is not pleased with me jumping up and down on the bed being cross and frustrated.

She says there are actual nicerer ways to wake up.

April 27

The previously ginger one has binned to the doctors and has gotted some new tablets. Happarently, they might do making her fat wot she is wailing about, but they should also stop her finking that everyfing is frightening, and stop her hearing fings wot aren't being said.

Mum wants to know if there is an opposite tablet for Dad; one that makes him hear fings which *are* being said before she has to get seriously frightening.

April 28

Today, I has been being a blinking numpty about hinvestigating my hoperation, *and* I has been trying to do lickering.

Peoples have been saying to Mum that I should be wearing a buster collar. Mum did try this and she now says that anyboddedy who finks they can hachieve this fing is welcome to come and try. Otherwise they can do keeping their flipping advices to themselves. I are not good a-very-tall about having fings near my neck fiddled with, so it was never going to be a hoption.

Sally-the-Vet said to use a basket muzzle instead. I did kindly decline Mum's kind offer of this, though, and went and hidded in the garden and did running away from her every time she came near me. But not in a cheeky Wooface kind of way; in a terrified-leave-me-alone-you scary-mum kind of way.

Mum was very hupset and wisely gived up.

I did decide to say hello to the previously ginger one. She is a mad cat lady and do never get hinvolved in fiddling about with actual me, so I did fink I was safe saying hello-Mum-is-being-actual-horrid-mean-to-me.

Turns out I was very wrong. I is suddenly wearing the muzzle. And the previously ginger one is looking very smug. She is a trickster, traitor-meany, and I are finking about never speaking to the previously ginger one ever, hever again.

April 29

Mum says seeing as I won't leave my hoperation alone, and can wriggle my tongue through the cage muzzle, and she's already stayed up all night with me once to make sure I don't do lickering it, I has got no choice. I has got to wear a buster collar. Those puffy ring collars are all very well and good, but I has gotted the longest tongue in the whole wide world, and I are too bendy for my own good. So they don't work.

It's all very actual okay for her but has you ever tried to do eating a doughnut without lickering your lips? And then staying like that for days when it is all itchy and sticky, and really, wheely needing to be cleaned up? That is wot is does feel like so I aren't speaking to anyboddedy. Especially people called Mum. And I aren't going in a car. And I aren't going to see Sally-the-Vet. And MOST OF ALL, I aren't getting castrated EVER, HEVER again. Mum says that's one thing we can be sure of.

I are wondering wot she means ...

BUSTER COLLARS

This isn't a poem about buster collars

And how horrid they is to wear

Cos I can't find the words

To tell of the hell

If I'm not allowed to swear.

April 30

Seeing as I can't bring myself to write an actual poem about this Orrendous Hexperience I has decided to write a Norror Story hinstead. Here goes.

Once-a very-pon-a-time there was a dog called Worzel Wooface, who did have a horrid Mum who did put a hateful buster collar on actual him.

Worzel did not want the buster collar on so he did bash it and scrape it and paw it, but it would not flipping blinking come off. And then he did scare himself quite actual silly, bashing into walls and making himself quite very terrified with all the noises, and not being able to see behind him.

So, Worzel Wooface went and hidded in the garden under the hedge. And did do snapping at everyboddedy who did try to get him to come inside again. Then he did go on actual hunger strike, and refuse to do eatering with the buster collar on. His horrid, hateful Mum could just about actual live with this for a day. But then Worzel did also decide to not do drinkering with the buster collar on, and every time someboddedy did come near him with a small bowl of water, he did running away and hiding again, bashing the buster collar on the banisters and freaking himself out again and again.

Heventually, the stupid hoomans did have to take off the buster collar or Woo would do dying of thirst, or his Mum would do dying of a broken heart, or Sally-the-Vet would have to put Mum on speed dial.

THE END

I are consentering to wear the basket muzzle now when I are not being supervised. Hanyfing is betterer than that buster collar. The whole very fing has been quite actual traumatic, and I has taken several steps backwards in trusting peoples, but we is all hopeful I will start to get over it quite very actual soon.

I are lying on Mum's bed, wearing the basket muzzle, and very actual hignoring Mum sitting in the doorway with water dripping out of her hiballs.

54

MAY

May 1

Dear Gipsy-the-Foster-Fridge

****HIMPORTANT HURGENT HINFORMATION****

I need to do telling you all about the Time Has Come and Do Somefing About It stuff.

It's a hoperation.

In my case they did chopping off most of my gentleman bits, but as you doesn't have gentleman bits, I has no idea wot your hoperation will be about. Happarently, it's all about stopping there being even more puppies in the world when there is billions of dogs waiting in rescues and hateful pounds for their forever homes. I do actual fink this is an exerlent actual idea, and do not be wanting to be adding to the problem. That bit is all very quite good, the hoperation is all very actual nuffink to worry about, but you might feel a bit sore and sleepy for a few days.

How-very-ever, you need to know that there is buster collar hinvolvement afterwards wot you need to make sure does not come anywhere actual very near you or your house. If you sees one you must do your bestest squashing it that I know you can do if you put your actual bottom to it. Wotever happens, make sure that they do not put one on you. They is Orrendous and Hateful, and I did do all sorts of snapping and growling, cos it did frighten me so actual very much.

And then Mum did leaking water from her hiballs and Dad did have to do lots of coping and looking after Mum and Me. Which he is very rubbish at when he'd rather be clicking Uff the Confuser.

We did nearly run out of wine.

I hope this is very actual useful hinformation, and that you does putting to very quite good use.

You has binned warned.

From your luffly boykin

Worzel Wooface

May 2

Peoples keep knockering on our door wanting to talk about how Mum and Dad are going to vote, cos there is a Helection coming up.

When there is a helection, some people do try to get choosed to be actual In Charge of everyboddedy else. It is all very confuddling but Mum says it goes a bit like this: some peoples will offer to give you lots of liver cake and some peoples will want to give you lots of cheese, and you do have to decide whether you want cheese or liver most-of-very-all, cos you can only have one or the other.

The most himportant fing about helections is the colours. There are a few to choose from. Wot colour you choose decides who is going to be

In Charge. Up here, lots of the fields seem to like blue. Mum says sheep aren't allowed to vote, and she do wonder if the blue people know this. Dad says lots of peoples who like the red colour don't bother to vote, which is just as bad. There are other colours like purple and yellow and green, but where I live it's mainly red and blue.

Dogs do not have helections. Where I do live we do not need to have an helection cos we do all know that even though Pip has moved to the next village, she is still In Charge, and there is no actual point in discussing it.

Also dogs are not very actual good at telling the difference between colours, so we could not have a very good helection anyway.

I fink the most himportant fing these peoples who are knocking on the door need to know is that noboddedy in this house will vote for anyboddedy who forgets to shut the blinking gate, wot keeps happening, and it's driving Dad bonkers.

May 3
Fings has been a bit actual calmer and reasonababble today. Mum has just about stopped sobbing, and Dad finks she might start pulling-herself-together-and-be-a-responsibabble-pet-owner quite actual soon. Seeing as Dad can't put flea drops on the cats without panickering he's hurting them, I did fink that maybe he shouldn't doing saying this where Mum could hear him. He did do taking my advices on this fing ...

I did wear the cage muzzle fing overnight, and this morning everyfing is looking much very betterer, and I aren't trying to fiddle about with my hoperation, so I has not had to wear nuffink plastic or freak-out-scary all day. I are refusing to breathe any sighs of relief until that cone of shame buster collar blinking flipping fing is safely in the bin, though. It's still in the kitchen. Just in Case.

May 4
This morning, I can't see any sign of the buster collar in the kitchen, so I are mostly feeling quite actual safer and happier. We is all hoping I will be quite very staying that way!

May 5
Yesterday, because I was feeling much betterer, I did helping Dad in the garden.

I actual quite love gardening, though Mum says wot I do is destructering and not gardening. Dad hates gardening. Not as much as he hates decky-rating but very nearly, so Mum has to convince him it's construction work, and not gardening or he will not be doing it.

She spends quite a lot of time trying to persuade me *not* to do gardening, and almost as much time trying to persuade Dad *to* do it.

I fink me and Mum would get on quite actual betterer if she did hunderstand wot I are trying to achieve in the garden.

****MY FORTS ON GARDENING****

- It tooked me ages to dig all them holes. Please don't be filling them in.
- You let me out in the garden to do weesandpoos. It shouldn't be a surprise if you step on somefing you don't like.
- Hanging baskets is the place to put plants you really, wheely don't want me to dig up. Anyfing else is going to be a bit variable.
- I cannot tell the difference between a path and a border; so telling me to 'get off' is a bit pointless.
- Given that I are a very quite picky eater wot finks peas are scary, I aren't likely to want to eat the plants in the garden. Tell Gran-the-Dog-Hexpert to stop having hystericals.
- Please put the rake away ... that wasn't funny.
- I aren't going in the garden if you are using that yellow snake fing that spits water.
- When I want to get somefing out of my tummy, any grass will do, even your fancy stripy posh stuff.
- That mole is mine.
- You can have the hedgehog.

May 8

Today, I carried on with my very epically-constructed-nearly-got-that-blinking-mole-I'll-have-'im-by-June trap.

The previously ginger one reckons I are too late. She looked out of the bedroom window this morning and the man with the perfick lawn opposite has got a fuge molehill in the middle of it.

Now, neither me OR the man with the not-quite-so-perfick lawn opposite are quite actual happy a-very-tall.

May 11

Today, Mum has hadded a My-Grain. A My-Grain is a type of hurted head that makes you need to lie down in a dark room and want to be dead.

My-Grains get triggered by fings; Mum has been wondering if it was the four hours she spended wandering around without her sunglasses on, or the oranges and chocolate she hadded after dinner, or the not-getting-enough-sleep or the sleeping-with-the-window-shut or the fuge stress and worry about Worzel Wooface and the hoperation wot triggered it. When she did finking about it like this, she called herself an actual plonker.

I has been an exerlent Nurse Wooface. I did lying on the bed very actual quite concerned all afternoon, and did not do hogging all the bed or turning hupside down and wobbling all over the actual place. I did not even do any sneaky bottom burps wot I do try to get a-very-way-with when I can.

Everyboddedy is quite actual himpressed with me. I do fink I are a saint, hespecially as Mum kept grabbing and rubbing her head and her eyes. I shoulda putted a buster collar on her to stop her fiddling ...

May 12

Now that I am betterer from my hoperation and have dunned forgiving everyboddedy for the hateful buster collar, Mum says we're going Back to Basics, and I are going to have to re-learn all the fings I decided not to bother with when I was being too hindependent for my own actual good.

Mum's made a list of all the fings I used to be reliababble about doing. I fink this is most actual unfair. I can do all kinds of other himportant and useful fings like sleep hupside down and do staying home alone without mainly chewing other people's hexpensive stuff or the carpet. And I do make Dad laugh every day when he comes home from work and ask for cuddles and a chat. I are fabumazing at stopping the cats pinching stuff, and chewing wellies is somefing I could do for a compertition. If there was a compertition for it ...

Mum says these fings are all wonderful and why she loves me so much, but I need to be safe when we is out for a walk if I want to do being let off my lead in public, and not make her look like a complete plonker. Or, more himportantly, not get hit by a car or get lost or stolen or any of those seriously freaky, frightening nightmare fings that keep Dad up at night when Mum is panickering and having hystericals about how she would feel if anything Happened. To. Worzel.

> **HIMPORTANT FINGS I USED TO BE ABLE TO DO**
> - Stop
> - Wait
> - Come - if I have to
> - Check back
> - Watch Mum
> - Sit - hoccasionally with a lot of sulking
>
> **FINGS I CAN RELIABABBLY DO AT THE MOMENT**
> - Nuffink

Today we has started with 'Watch Mum,' and it's all binned a great success, although I has no actual idea wot we've binned doing, to be very quite honest. All I know is that every time I has looked at Mum, I've binned told I is a good boy, and sometimes gived a fishy treat. It's all binned quite very relaxed and fishy-tasting.

And progress, happarently.

May 13

Mum knows that I are very rubbish at responding to pressure. If I is asked to do somefing worrying, I fink about it too actual much and do running away and hiding. So everyfing *she* wants me to do, I has to fink is all my own clever and cunning idea. And I aren't all that very hinterested in treats. I quite often worry that I are being bribed or going to get tolded off for somefing cos I was tricked and smacked and hurt when I was a ickle baby puppy for all sorts of fings I didn't hunderstand.

So, today, sometimes when I looked at Mum, she said 'Watch me,' and after yesterday and getting all the luffly strokes and sometimes a fishy, I did not find this too actual complercated or frightening, and I did decide that it was very okay to look at her without running away. I are getting mighty sick of fishies, though, and are hoping Mum will remember about cheese very quite actual soon!

May 14

Mum decided to try and have another go with a clicker today, and even though she had cheese to go with the clicks, it wented about as well as it did a year ago. I do not like clicks, and I do not respond to clicks. Well, I do. I hear a click and I run away and hide, which is probababbly not wot I are supposed to do according to the hinstructions from the Dog Hexpert, and on the back of the clicker packet and on Google. So I fink we can safely actual say that I is about as clicker trained as I are ever going to be. I hear it. I run away.

May 16

I eated the clicker. All over the bed and under the duvet. When Dad got into bed tonight, it didn't click, it crunched. And then he yelled like wot you might do if you stooded on a piece of lego in the middle of the night. Or sat down on a bed and gotted lumps of sharp plastic himbedded in your bum.

I has binned hejected from the bedroom and has got to sleep on the sofa tonight. I aren't too very happy about this, and I fink I are in the Doghouse, but is has all binned very quite worth it because the clicker is in the bin!

May 17

My walk today was very slow. You know wot it is like when you've binned on your hollibobs, and come back to a fuge pile of letters and loads of hemails? Well, that was wot my walk was actual like. So many doggies had lefted me messages along the bee-strip wot the farmer has lefted along the side of one of the fields to get hinsects to visit his crops, where I do often walk, and I had to check out them all, and leave a reply, as very well.

Mum tooked advantage of me checking all my messages to do some more of the Watch Me stuff wot I fink went quite very well. It was very actual easier for her to do this cos I wasn't three fields away playing with pigeons, she says. One of the reasons I might have been less keen on bogging off (apart from dealing with all the messages along the path) is that I have losted some of my fitness after a three-week layoff. I has losted some weight from being a bit poorly-sick, and sulking as well. I tried some running and fort about chasing a crow, but I was actual rubbish at it and gotted all puffed out. I will need to be doing some more hexercise over the next few weeks, I fink.

THE MAGIC WORD

Hoomans have a magic word
To get the fings they need
Like cuppateas and lifts back
home
And sparkly dresses they've
seed

Manners are himportant
fings
For little girls and boys
So they is taught a special
word
To say to get noo toys

Dogs don't have a magic word
We don't fink much of
'please'
If you want a sit or down
You'll have to find some
cheese

All the pleases in the world
And asking with a smile
Will not get a stay or fetch
Or 'wait there for a while'

The bestest way to get a dog
To come back like a rocket
Is to check you've always got
Some cheese in your back
pocket

We doggies will not work for
free
Or sit cos you said 'please'
So my advices to you all ...
Get out the smelly cheese!

May 18

It's Gypsy-was-Pandy-the-Foster-Fridge's Gotcha Day today! A Gotcha Day is a quite very special day in the life of a rescue dog. It's probably the most actual very himportant day of their lives cos it's the day when they move to be with their forever famberly and start their new life. We has binned sent super pictures of Gypsy enjoying her liver cake and trying to sit on her Mum's head, and everyboddedy looking really, wheely happy!

But fings is not quite so actual happy here. Mum's realised that it's been a whole year since she started nagging Dad about mending the banisters wot me and Gypsy did break, and he *still* hasn't fixed them. They're still wobbling and creaking and looking like they'll fall down any minute. When Mum realised that it's been a whole year and still nuffink has been dunned, she did start lookering round at all the other fings wot Dad hasn't fixed. Like the front of the dishwasher and the warbrobe door. All of this is very not being a proper Man About The House, happarently. Dad says seeing as Mum won't stop nagging him, he's not going to be a Man About The House, a-very-tall. He's going to be a Man Aboard His Boat. In the harbour. With his dog.

May 21

It's Gandhi's birfday today. He is a whole year old, and is a proper growed-up cat! He and Frank seem to do forgetting this fing all the actual time, though, and do proper kitten biff-and-bash playing. I aren't allowed to join in with these games and have to do waiting my turn otherwise Frank gets quite very cross and jealous. And then I do chasing him out of the catflap when Gandhi isn't lookering. Then Gandhi is lefted sitting on the kitchen floor wondering if he's been himagining biffing Frank up. And where he's gone, and why the honly fing lefted to be biffed is my tail hanging down where Frank used to be!

May 22

When Hazel-Hattie did do being fostered here, she did get all over-hexcited and eat my bed, and pulled all the fluff out of the hinsides so it is more like a ground sheet that a proper bed now. Mum says I did deserve a noo bed as a treat for being luffly to Hazel-Hattie I do not fink I has binned gived a treat. I has given the noo bed a bit of a sniff, and I even did do lying down next to it, but I do not like it so I are hignoring the noo bed. Mum says she is working very actual hard at hignoring me, hignoring the noo bed.

I am now hiding at the top of the landing pretending the noo bed doesn't hexist. Happarently, I are resistant to change. And a Ludd-Ite,

Sometime soon I are hexpecting Mum to announce that she has boughted Gandhi a new bed.

May 23

After a very long time of hignoring the bed and Mum hignoring me, hignoring the bed, last night I did find some ickle fishies, wot are my bestest treat, hidded in it. So I had a bit of a sniff and found some of my old bed in amongst the new one as well. I gave it a bit of a nudge and a prod and, before I knewed it, it wasn't a scary noo bed for Gandhi but my luffly noo, very quite large and actual comfy bed wot does need some serious work to get it quite right but it's mine. Not Gandhi's.

When you is a doggy, you can do changing your mind, and everyboddedy do say you are very quite clever and a good actual boy. And not a numpty wot was being a total wally.

May 25

I are very quite actual pleased to hannounce that, despite my hoperation, I can still do cocking my leg like a proper boykin. Mum finks I seem to be a bit calmer and keener to stay around her, but now I has also gotted a better idea about these treat fings, it is difficult to say whether it's the treats or the hoperation.

Noboddedy seems to care much, to be actual honest. They is just glad I aren't bogging off into the distance all the blinking time.

May 26

Mum says her Back to Basics work is going very actual well. She has all these treats and stuff in her pockets wot she keeps stuffing down my neck whenever I look at her or come back to her. Sometimes, though, I do grab the fishy-treat and then do belting around with it in my mouth. Mum doesn't mind cos then I come back for another one and do it again.

Although I are a bit hinterested in the treats in Mum's pockets I still aren't wot you'd call treat-oriented. And frowing toys mostly completely confuddles me. Very quite occasionally I'll take one for a trip round the fields, but I has to be feeling quite actual over-hexcited and silly to do that.

Today, I did do that silly fing and then I dropped the yellow ring in amongst the sugar beet. And now I can't find it. I hadded a good proper look, and even Merlin joined in the hunt, but it has goned. Mum reckons there are about a dozen toys in that field now, and could I please do holding onto them a bit actual betterer before she has to take out a loan.

Back to Basics seems to be about Team Work. About me and Mum having the same ideas about wot we want to do. So long as we is in agreement about that fing, then everyboddedy is very actual happy. One fing Mum has learnt is that when I has a proper walk every single day I are quite very good at the Back to Basics fing. If we has to skip a proper walk, then the next day I are not so good at doing the team work fing, and I are not so good at the Watch ME and Wait cos I are too hexcited to concentrate on remembering about Mum.

May 27

This terribibble two stuff seems to be causing Merlin all kinds of actual bother as well at the moment, and he hadded his gentleman bits trimmed over a year ago, so it can't be that wot is causing the troubles.

Merlin's founded out he's got a nose, happarently. I aren't sure this is actual right cos I fink he's probababbly knowed this for quite a very long time. But he's worked out how to use it and it's driving Louise, his mum, Completely. Bonkers. But on our walks, Merlin has founded out that he can smell rabbits and pheasants and other small hanimals, HAND he can sniff out where they has goned. So he puts his nose to the ground and shoots off after the smells.

It seems that Merlin's ears and nose can't do working at the same actual time. If he is sniffing he can't hear his Mum yelling at him to come back. It all sounds very quite like me as well. When I see somefing, I can't hear nuffink. Wot with Pip shrieking and barking and hignoring Louise's pleas to stop talking so much, HAND Hazel's food fetish, I fink I has maded a himportant sigh-an-triffic discovery!

It seems that when we doggies get to be nearly growed up, our ears stop working when we don't fink we need them. When I are seeing, and Pip is yelling or Merlin is sniffing, and Hazel-Hattie is bin-raiding, we need ears like a hole in the head. Which is wot ears actual are, if you fink about it. And cos we don't need holes in the head, our ears close up so we can't hear nuffink. Which is why hoomans do fink we is hignoring them. It's not our fault; it's our ears.

May 29

There's a fuge problem with this Back to Basics stuff. Dad. Some hinteresting hadventures, and actual not doing as I are asked have happened when Dad and I are out on a manly walk. This has Got. To. Change. Mum says he has got to get much betterer at seeing wot's happening up ahead, and doing this 'Watch me' stuff and not talking to Worzel about the bits of the boats that need fixing, and wot he'd do if he was the manager of Leeds Football Club. Otherwise, Dad will undo all of Worzel's and Mum's hard work.

Dad's decided that the bestest fing he can do is find a safe field and do playing with me when we do go out on our own. Dad is much, much betterer at playing with me than Mum, mainly cos there are so many bits broken on Mum that just walking in a straight line is an hachievement.

Today, me and Dad did fabumazing scary chase in the water meadow, and we both gotted quite actual soggy. And I didn't do bogging off or nuffink, even though I gotted very, very over-hexcited!

Mum reckons this is all exerlent. 'Watch me' is really all about being far very more hinteresting than going on a hexplore or chasing pigeons, and no wonder I've binned bogging off if Dad's been boring me to death with complercated talk about the muck on the bottom of the boat, or how rubbish Leeds are. She would have runned away, too. And dunned refusing to come back ...

May 30

Mum and Louise did haccidentally discover the solution to the ears-stopping-working-hole-in-the-head fing today.

Merlin was about to do shooting off after a bunny, and I was about to do chasing a crow, when Mum putted her foot in the wrong actual place, sunk down about a foot into some mud ... and felled over. And made a fuge blinking great noise about it. Then Louise sawed wot Mum had dunned and started laughing, and tried to pull Mum out of the mud, and they was making such a kerfuffle that me and Merlin couldn't help but force our ears to work to find out wot the blinking heck they were squealing about. Cos it was a most quite very hawful noise wot you couldn't do hignoring if you actual wanted to! Suddenly, their mud-wrestling, pant-peeing hysticals were very much more hinteresting than anyfing me and Merlin had founded, so we wented back to hinvestigate. Heven Pip shutted up and stood there wondering whether it would be helpful to digger them out of the mud.

So Mum's worked it out: every time it looks like I are about to bog off into the distance, she's just got to do rolling around in the mud, screaming and having laughing hysticals. She's not keen.

May 31

The previously ginger one has binned learning about Florry's Tree. Dad and the fuge ginger boyman do keep calling it flower arranging, and getting very told off by the previously ginger one cos it's actual much more than that, and they make her sound like a lady-wot-lunches who does decky-rating churches. Which she is not. Turns out the previously ginger one is very quite good at Florry's Tree, and so she is trying to teach Mum about it, too.

Mum's rubbish at it. She loves it and is always very proud and pleased with wot she makes, but she is very actual useless. For some reason I cannot work out, Mum likes to sing and dance around whilst she's doing her Florry's Tree, and gets all very over-hexcited channelling wot she calls her creative juices. The previously ginger one ends up with her head on the kitchen table muttering that Mum's a nutter and pleading with her to follow the rules, wot are himportant, and could she actual Stop. Singing. so she can tell her the next bit. Then Frank comes to join in.

Frank is not wot you'd call helpful at Florry's Tree. He is very actual hinterested in checking out all the flowers and chewing on anyfing he finks is hedible, but mostly swishes all the leaves and bits of green spongy stuff onto the floor with his hincredibly long tail. Then Gandhi bats the bits of green stuff around the floor until it hexplodes, wot makes him sneeze.

After a couple of hours, Mum and the previously ginger one emerge from the kitchen. The previously ginger one has got a perfickly round and booful flower fing wot is all neat and correct, and has dunned following the rules. Mum's covered in green dust, got a hidiotic grin on her face, and has produced a fing that looks like every actual one of David Bowie's hairstyles rolled into one manic flower hexplosion.

Me and Dad are very actual keeping out of it all. Dad can't believe how much mess they make, and he's pretty actual certain that the ladies-wot-lunch don't destroy their kitchens doing flower arranging. Cos otherwise they wouldn't be able to cook lunch. Maybe that's the difference between flower arranging and Florry's Tree.

JUNE

June 1

Today we practiced STOP. Stop is quite very hard to practice cos you has to be going somewhere to stop. Fortunately, I has not yet got my fastest deaf-ear-clamping, wind-whizzing speed back since my hoperation, but I sawed a pheasant and I was off as fast as I could go. Mum was worried cos, half a mile away, there was a road at the end of the path I was shooting along, so she yelled 'Stop!' And then started doing some kind of hysterical yelling and whooping and dancing stuff. It was all very quite the same to the time she felled in the mud and losted her wellie.

Half a mile might sound like a long way, and a bit actual hexcessive for a stopping distance, but the fing with Sighthounds is that by the time anyboddedy says the 'St ...' bit of 'Stop,' we can be 200 yards away! And not listening any actual more, so you has to be quick. And loud.

I don't know wot Stop! means. And I definitely don't know wot the dancing is about, but the way Mum shoutered 'Stop!,' all scaredy-sounding, and then the yelling and himpression of Julie Andrews on the top of a mountain, was quite very actual difficult to hignore. So I stopped, and when she said 'Wait,' I did some more finking and gettering over being puffed out until she caughted up with me, so we could do deciding wot to do next. Mum said I was a luffly, clever boykin and offered me a treat, which I did not actual want, though I was very quite pleased with all the ruffles and strokes, so I didn't notice my lead being put on.

Mum hopes that, heventually, I'll just stop when she says 'Stop!' without her having to pretend she's being attacked by a swarm of wasps whilst singing Abba songs, cos otherwise people might fink she's a bit odd. But it'll do for now. In the middle of a field, miles away from anyfing where noboddedy can see her making a total twonk of herself, just so I don't bog off.

She says she's almost, completely, *nearly* sure I are worth it.

I still don't have wot you'd call a reliababble recall, though. Coming back is not somefing I are keen on. I'll do exerlent come-in-Mum's-general-direction and then go straight past, or I'll do come-to-within-ten-feet-but-not-close-enuff-to-have-the-lead-on. Which is mainly cos I don't WANT to go back on my blinking lead. I are having too much actual fun and want to carry on! Seems pretty flipping hobvious to me.

But seeing as we've got Stop and Wait pretty much horganised now, Mum reckons my recall is bearababble. I will do come-near-enuff. Then I will do Wait. And then Mum will walk towards me, give me a treat or a luffly, ruffly stroke, and then I will have my lead clipped on. And not to do much actual hobjectoring cos I are usually panting and puffing and ready for a bit of a rest.

June 2

I do know that some doggies like to do that 'come' fing where they do sit and then stick their noses between their hoomans legs, but that is never going to work for me. Or for Mum, to be quite very honest, cos unless she's planning on growing eight inches in the next actual day or so, my nose is never, ever, hever going to go in that space unless I are lying down. Or she is standing on a box.

Dad says he is very quite relieved that this is not hessential. If it was he would be having serious actual second forts about whether he ever wanted to risk taking Worzel Wooface for another walk, cos a Sighthound running straight at him at forty miles an hour, then punching him in the goolies with his nose is only going to end in a Opital visit. We has decidered to stick with 'Wait.'

June 4

Mum went to visit Willow today. Willow is wot the stray cat who moved into our shed, and then into the house and then maded five kittens, is called nowadays. When she was at our house, we did spend a lot and a lot of time worrying about her being a too-young mummy cat: she was skinny and ickle, and we all did fink that it was going to be too very much for her tiny boddedy. But somehow she managed to do a fabumazing job of being a mummy cat. And she maded Gandhi who is my bestest cat and Onorary Lurcher, so I fink she is special and himportant.

My famberly did a lot of finking, deciding wot was best for Willow's forever home, and for a little bit, they did fink about her becoming part of our famberly. But Dad had a bit of a panic about the fort of having six cats, and Gipsy, our senior cat, was quite very actual unfriendly to her. Just when we were starting to have a worry about finding her a forever home, cos she wasn't a cute ickle kitten but a very quite scruffy skinny mess, to be actual quite honest, she was offered the most perfick forever home, hever, and everyboddedy did big sighs of relief.

Willow lives quite very near to us, though far enuff away not to fink about coming to visit us on her own. Seeing as how she's got three whole acres of wild area, and a duck pond, HAND her own personal sundeck, I aren't really surprised she's quite very happy where she is. Most actual himportant of all, she is luffed and looked after, and very allowed to carry on being a proper hunting, hindependent cat. And she looks just like Gandhi now, not a skinny mess a-very-tall. She is quite short and plump and probababbly full of baby bunnies like him as actual well.

June 5

Mum's just remembered cats have anal glands. I shan't tell you hexactly how she did come to remember, but she says she will be picking up Mouse for a cuddle much, much more actual carefully in future.

June 6

Me and Mum has binned robberdobbed! Dad says he has quite an actual lot of simperfy for me and none a-very-tall for Mum cos she's so blinking useless at remembering stuff, it's amazing she makes it home every day with the car. And me. Mum put her bank card in a machine in a shop and then forgotted to take it out. So, some hidiot wented all around a big town using her money to get drunk! Which was pretty blinking stoopid cos all the pubs do have cameras in them and he's gonna get caught by the police peoples.

My robberdobbing is far more actual blinking serious, and I has not gotted any police peoples who is going to help me, wot I do fink is quite very actual unfair. And wrong. And I is not happy.

My ear feathers has goned. Dis-a-very-peared! And I want to know who has gotted them. I did love my ear feathers very actual much. They were fabumazing for hanging burrs from and for tickling Mum's nose with, and very actual exerlent for teasing Gandhi. I has had a good check and they has definitely goned. When I do find out who has nickered them, they is going to have some hexplaining to do ...

June 7

Do not be telling Gran this but I are getting pretty good at that showing-off-hobedience milarky. You mustn't tell Gran-the-Dog-Hexpert cos she'll get all over-hexcited, and do finking that 'there's hope for Worzel yet.'

There isn't. There is habsolutely no blinking chance I are jumping over some complercated hobstacle in the hope of half a sausage 'sometimes.' But if I are asked nicely without anyboddedy watching, and with no prickles of nasty gravel hunder me, I will consider doing sit, wait ... (be lookering round to make sure Merlin isn't sniggering at actual me from the bushes) ... wait ... and ... OFF you go! But, like I said, do NOT be telling the Dog-Hexpert.

June 9

The fuge ginger boyman has dunned all his exams for his first year at Universally and is waiting for the results so he can start breathing again. He finks he's dunned okay, but Universally isn't like school where you get tolded hexactly where you are and wot you need to do cos they do assuming you are a hadult, and you is hexpected to be hindependent and a growed-up. Mum says that it was honly yester-actual-day that he was a baby, and couldn't say the word 'yellow,' so she's struggling with this hadult fing quite a very lot.

The rest of us aren't worried about him being a hadult; we're wondering if he's binned hinvaded by aliens cos since he gotted his house all sorted and ended up being putted in charge of all the horganising, he's becomed all very hinterested in gardening – gardening, of all fings! The last time the fuge ginger boyman showed any hinterest in gardening was in 1996, when he could just about walk, and then he was more hinterested in sitting in a wheelbarrow and eating mud. Now he's asking Mum for spare forks and other diggering stuff cos he wants to grow flowers in his garden, and make it all very actual pretty.

Worzel Wooface

He's even asking Mum how to chop back roses properly so they doesn't die.

Mum says she don't fink he's binned hinvaded by aliens; it's in his jeans, this gardening bug. Everyboddedy in our famberly gets this bug when they become a growed-up, she says. And maybe, Mum finks, he might be one of those independent hadult fings wot can pass exams without their Mum nagging them after-very-all.

June 10

I went for a fuge walk and playtime with Lola today, and I has got to say that I fink Lola's Mum, Jill, is a bit actual mean about Lola. Jill finks Lola is a bit, well, de-fish-ent in the brains department but I does not fink this is true – and I has hevidence.

Brains is wot you must use if you are wanting to catch me. Without brains, you will not do cutting corners and sneakering up behind me. Lola does fabumazing sneakering-up-behind-me, so I do fink Lola's Mum is not happreciating her brains a-very-nuff. Either that, or I are getting slow in my old age but I do not fink that is a true fact. The grass was very quite long, though. Lola wiggles and squiggles through the grass, but I does prefer to bounce on the top of it, so I spends quite a lot of time going up rather than along.

My ears do not be helping with hairy-dymanics of trying to stay on top of the grass. My legs bounce up at the same time as my ears bounce down, so I are all over the place, and going up and down and forward all at the same time, which is not good for being speedy. Mum says I look blinking hilarious, which is quite actual rude, but I do suffering this cos all the time I are looking funny, Mum isn't finking about time to go home and work out wot to cook for dinner, and whether Dad will have forgotted to remember for the billionth time to bring her shoes off the boat.

June 11

We saw a little toad on our walk today. He was a toad on a mission because he was walking down a track. He did hobviously know where he was going, like lots of toads actual do at this time of year.

I are saying 'he' but I don't actual know how to tell the difference between a boy toad and a girl toad. So I could be really hoffending him. I mean her. Erm ...

Hanyway, I was a very exerlent boykin at hobserving the toad from behind Mum and not frightening the toad, and Worzel-could-you-come-a-little-bit-closer-so-I-can-take-a-blinking-photo-it's-not-going-to-eat-you. I did that bit brilliantly but in the end I did hagree to take a couple of steps closer so Mum could do bending down to take the photo.

I are careful. And cautious. And good fings like that. And I are Not. A. Wimp. like wot Mum did call me.

June 14

I did somefing very quite gob-smacking today. Mum says so. And she hasn't stopped telling everyboddedy about it all day. There's a fuge ditch wot runs right down the middle of one of my bestest fields. It's a old stream wot has binned carved and dugged out to be a drainage ditch. There's never enuff water to make it look like a river or a stream, but when I do go in it, I come out all wet and muddy and sticky. And cos it's binned dugged out, it has very actual steep sides, so going for a quick swim and squish about in it is a fabumazing idea ... until you need to do gettering out. You can probabably guess that I did do this fing once and it didn't end well for anyboddedy. Hespecially Dad, who had Mum squeaking 'Do Somefing!' at him, and me having to use him as a lumpy kind of ladder to get out of the ditch.

When we were walking today I missed the grassy bridge that do let me be on the same side as Mum, and founded myself quite actual stucked on the wrong side. Now, the sensibibble fing would have binned to go belting back to the grassy bridge, cross it, then caughted up with Mum. But I did not have my sensibibble head on. I had my panic-panic-stuck-and-worried head on. So I ranned round and round in little circles for a bit, and then up and down the bank for a bit, and then ... I just launched myself right over the ditch, which Mum reckons is at least fifteen feet wide. And I did not land in the middle of it with a squelch and a splash and a fump. I did actual land on the other side, and honly needed to do a teeny-tiny bit of scrabbling to be back with Mum. Who just stooded there with her mouth hanging open like the hatch to the loft.

June 15

Today I are TWO! And before anyboddedy do ask, I are not having a party or anyfing special or worrying happening. I don't like surprises and hunexpected fings, so today my famberly and me is having Worzel's Perfick Day, wot will be very quite predictababble and all about wot I like doing bestest, with no sudden cakes or other strange, scaredy stuff. Some doggies like all that kind of fing and lots of attention and fuss but I. Do. Not. I like fings very quiet and simple. And no parties. Mum says I are getting more and more like blinking Dad every day.

Worzel's Perfick Day did start on the bed. Hupside down with Mum and Dad having a cuppatea and me rolling about and trying to spill it everywhere. Then Mum did get up, and very most himportantly put on her wellies *straight away,* so I knew we was going for a walk. Outside, I did hear Pip and Merlin squeaking and barking, so I knew they was coming with us, so I did lots of jumping up and down on the bed trying to see them. (It's actual himpossible unless they do standing on stilts, but I do try and I are sure they can always hear the bed springs squeaking, even if Mum finks it is himpossible.)

We all did go for a fabumazing walk, and there was no stuff about please-don't-go-in-the-ditch-the-kitchen-floor-is-quite-clean-at-the-moment. And we did have lots of time for playing and running about, and a bit of Wooface following Merlin, following his nose, into the woods.

After breakfast I did getting myself cleaned up by rolling around on the ancient office carpet wot Mum's gived up about, followed by a long snooze whilst Mum did her bits of paperwork and confuser stuff.

In the afternoon, I wented down to the harbour to meet Dad from work, and we went for a blast about on the beach and into the sea. We stopped off at a pub on the way home where I did get offered lots of yummy snacks wot I mostly hignored, and Mum sighed and said 'it's-the-thought-that-counts,' and did giggling cos that's wot everyboddedy says on their birfdays.

At home, I had my favouritist chicken wings for dinner with no sneaky bits of other stuff wot might be good for me to pick around and dump on the carpet. Mum says dogs can't live on chicken wings alone, but she is quite very actual wrong about that. I could. I very actual could if I was allowed to, but I aren't cos it's not a balanced diet, happarently. But because it was my birfday we did forget about the balanced diet stuff and just do making Worzel happy, which is wot birfdays should be about, I fink. My last bit of Worzel's Perfick Day was all about a marry-thong session of watching telly and snoozing, with Dad shoutering at the men trying to kick their balls.

Usually I don't have two fuge walks in one day, so my birfday was quite actual special in that way. Mostly, though, I did wot I normally do every day. After all, it's tooked me two years to discover wot makes me quite very actual happy, which has been blinking quite actual hard work, wot with me starting off being worried about everyfing. And it turns out I like doing a lot of fings wot Mum and Dad do like doing. Which is a very actual good job cos Mum reckons if I'd discovered I like sky-diving, or somefing daft like that, she woulda struggled to join in!

June 16

Gran-the-Dog-Hexpert has gotted to hear about my fifteen-foot world record, nearly Worzel-breaking jump across the ditch and has begunned wittering on about me being perfick for doing Working Trials cos it 'hinvolves a fuge long jump wot I'd be able to do easily.'

I fink she's forgotted that there is other fings hinvolved in Working Trials, like working, for a start. And finding fings. I are rubbish at finding fings, and if the Dog-Hexpert finks I are perfick for working trials I are going to have to become even more actual rubbish at that fing. I are perfick for lying on the sofa, and I has got no intention of finding some strange fing in the middle of a ploughed field when it be raining. I are going to have to hide a few actual fings and then fail to find them big-time-badly so Mum forgets about this Working Trials idea wot the Dog-Hexpert has putted in her head ...

June 17

There will come an actual point in every dog's life when someboddedy will wonder if you is bored and need more hexcitement in your actual very life. Wot with my very quite hoptional recall and being far too hindependent for my own good, Mum's begunned to wonder if I need training classes, or a Hobby. I has to say that I are perfickly happy with the hobbies I has already got: chewing wellies and belting after crows are exerlent hobbies. But Mum's binned finking maybe I need somefing more actual structured. I has been trying quite actual hard to havoid all this stuff for over a year now, and I've gotted quite good at havoiding these fings.

*****TOP TIPS FOR HAVOIDING HOBBIES AND HOCCUPATIONS*****

- 🐾 The most actual himportant fing to remember is that, in most cases, Dad is not going to be helpful. Dad is after a quiet life, which mainly means keepering Mum busy with fings so she doesn't remember he needs to fix the car or learn how to speak Spanish. With her. At a class with other people who he Hasn't Met and Doesn't Want to Meet, in the Village Hall where it's freezing. And Leeds are playing football on the telly. So, he will be quite actual hencouraging for you to do a Hobby with Mum and leave him to have a quiet life.

- 🐾 If you do hear a click, Run, Away. Even if the click seems to be coming from a yummy bit of cheese or sausage. There is somefing about that click which is like brain-actual-washing, and soon you'll want to walk on one leg, just to hear a click. It's like a haddiction.

- 🐾 Sit - this is to be havoided at all costs. Once you has agreed to do Sit, hoomans will try their luck with Down. Then they'll get all hexcited, and before you know it, they'll be finking you can load the washing machine. And suddenly, you is cleverer than most Dads. If you never let it get past Sit, you will not find yourself on the slippery-slidey-slope that leads from deckrative to useful. Being useful is one of the most himportant and hessential Fings to Havoid.

- 🐾 That is not to say that you should be bad or unhelpful. Not lying in doorways and letting hoomans go up the stairs and staying inside the garden will create the himpression that you is 'good enuff' and nice to live with. If you is always very quite blinking naughty you could find yourself at training classes where you will be under ignormous pressure to do Sit. Cos everyboddedy else is.

- 🐾 Only ever dead one glove, or chew one boot on a bed. Or hide one sock. If you start collecting fings in two-by-twos, peoples might start to fink that you can count. Terribibble fings happen to dogs wot can count. You fink you've got the idea of one and two. Suddenly, it's 'and-FIVE-6-7-8' and you're off to learn how to do heelwork to music, which is blinking actual dancing. Your dance partner will be your Mum, and you've seen her attempts at dancing after a drink of cider enuff times to know that it won't do ending well. Dad will be frilled to bits, though; for years he's been pretendering to have a bad knee to havoid doing dancing with your Mum, and suddenly you've replaced him!

- 🐾 Never, ever, hever volunteer to find stuff. You must keep it a fuge secret that you know hexactly where Mum's other wellie is (mainly cos it was you wot lefted it in the garden), and going to collect it won't do you any favours. I do realise you might have to miss out on a walk or two if your mum can't find her other wellie, but in the long run, it will be betterer. There are all kinds of himportant and dangerous real jobs for dogs wot can find stuff. Most of them hinvolve lookering for bombs or drugs attached to scaredy-looking people. Doing heroic stuff is hexausting, **HAND** involves finking. And also decidering if someboddedy is going to blow themselves up.

In my hopinion, loafering about on the sofa waiting for your dinner is a much actual betterer hobby than any of these actual very hoccupations, so I shall be carrying on with my cunning plan of doing Sit quite actual slowly, and lookering like I will faint every time I are asked to do it. It seems to be working so far.

June 18
My hiding and losing stuff plan has actual backfired. Mum says she is missing six shoes. Six *different* shoes. Happarently, I are the prime suspect and there will be no walks until I give them back. I do fink this is actual unfair.

Mum says she isn't being unfair; it's more of a practical problem. She quite very actual has No. Shoes. In. Pairs to put on her feets, and can't leave the house.

Fink I'd better go and get her wellie out of the garden and drop it somewhere very not hobvious where she might not have looked already, in case she finks I are super-smart. Or would be good at Working Trials.

June 20
I did not feel very actual well last night and I was sick. There was some blood in there as well so Mum phoned Sally-the-Vet to decide on A Plan of Action. And have a panic and some ferapy. Sally-the-Vet is actual nice like that and quite very used to Mum.

They do both fink that it was a combination of my worming tablet and me eating some grass wot did scratch my tummy, but as there is a nasty bug 'going round' near here at the very moment, they is not taking any actual chances.

Noboddedy does worrying like my Mum. Dad says that noboddedy else in the famberly needs to worry about anyfing cos Mum does enough worrying for all of us. And most of Ingerland, too, to be actual honest.

I are okay in myself, and doing bouncing about, but today I are on a light diet and gettering lots of luffly strokes. And being hobserved. Very, very hobserved. I aren't allowed to go anywhere without Mum trotting after me like my shadow to see wot I are doing.

June 21
I is definitely feeling much very betterer and everyfing is back to quite actual normal. Well, as normal as fings ever get round here ...

June 22
I gotted a toy piggywiggy from the previously ginger one today, wot she

reckons is fantastic because it goes 'oink' rather than the usual hyper-sonic squuuuueak noise that dog toys usually make. So noboddedy is going to plead with me to hurry up and dead the blinking squeaking fing, and who's-stupid-idea-was-it-to-buy-that-anyway?

Like with most toys, I was not very actual sure about it at first. When Dad gotted home from work, he did decide to show me how it worked by putting it in his mouth and crawlering up and down the hall with it. My Dad is fabumazing like that.

According to Mum, my Dad is 'highly respected in hindustry circles.' I can see why.

June 23

It turns out that 'oink' at two o'clock in the morning sounds like a Worzel Wooface being sick, coughing and choking. So me and Oink the Piggywiggy have to do playing hunder supervision from now on.

Not because Oink the Piggywiggy is dangerous or nuffink, but because Mum forgetting I are playing with it, and hurling herself down the stairs in a blind panic when she is half asleep, could end up being quite very actual lethal. For Mum.

****RULES ABOUT TOYS****

- 🐷 I want to play with toys only very sometimes, and only in the house or in the garden. Toys wot are taken on walks are likely to get lefted in the middle of the sugar beet field.
- 🐷 I cannot tell the difference between your toys and my toys.
- 🐷 I may prefer your toys to mine ... in very actual fact. I probababbly will.
- 🐷 I aren't actual sure wot the difference is between a shoe and a toy. Please can you hexplain again?
- 🐷 Anyfing left on the bed is a toy.
- 🐷 Even if it is hexpensive.
- 🐷 Knickers can be toys. And offered to visitors.
- 🐷 Just because you fink it is a lovely new toy. I may hate it. Sorry about that fing.
- 🐷 And go back to playing with the soggy lump of cardboard I founded in the garden.
- 🐷 I like it when you do playing toys with me. But if you look like you is having a fabumazing time, I may just to do watching you makering a plonker of your very actual self.

June 25

Today on my walk I did find a FING. It was a really, wheel disgustering fing wot Mum refused to hinvestigate too closely cos it was smelly and soggy. When I founded it, I did picking it up and taking it for a run around the field, with it flappering out of each side of my mouth. And then I did drop it, quite very much to Mum's relief cos she wanted me to Leave. It. And put-it-down-you-revolting-oaf. On the plus side, Mum said I was so hinterested in taking the smelly FING for a run that I was not a teeny-tiny bit hinterested in chasing all the crows wot did hexplode into the air when I runned past them.

June 27
Mum fort I had losted the FING, but I was very actual quite clever yesterday and lefted it in a safe place so that I could do rediscovering it again today. As a very actual bonus, I did also get to show Merlin the fing. His Mum was about as fond of the fing as my Mum. Merlin was very actual pleased with my exerlent discovery, and we both did take it for a trip round the field whilst Louise and Mum did an actual lot of drop-it-don't-bring-it-anywhere-near-me-you-revolting-dogs squeakering. We wasn't listening, we was too busy playing ...

June 28
Mum was hoping I would have forgotted about the Fing or a fox might have runned off with it during the night, but it was hexactly where I did leave it.

Because it is all squishy and mud-coloured (and very, very VERY dead-something-or-other-shaped) it sort of disappears into the muddy track, so once I has dropped it, a hooman would have to do very quite hard looking to find it. If you has got a doggy nose wot can sniff out yummy disgustering smells, then it's easy to find.

Mum wasn't himpressed, especially as we were practising sit, wait, wait, off you ... I didn't wait for the 'go.' I just wented and collected my fing and belted off. Mum's fishies and cheese are no compertition for a smelly fing. And she says she definitiely isn't ever, hever carrying around wot-ever-it-is in her pocket, even though she reckons I would do anyfing, hanyfing for a chance to play with it.

June 29
The fing is dead. Well, it was already dead to be quite actual honest, but now it is very deaded and quite actual goned. Mum grabbed it off Merlin, who was not very quick enuff to havoid this disaster, and then she Threw. It. In. Some. Stinging. Nettles. where none of us dogs was gonna go.

On our walk home, Mum kept holding her hand out to the side of her as if she did not want to have it attached to her boddedy. And she had to do very quite hard remembering not to touch her face or her mouth. And shuddering at the fort of it. I don't know why she was that actual worried; I've binned carrying it around in my mouth for the past five days, and slobberobbering all over it, and probababbly swallowing some of the loose bits wot have dropped off the fing, and nuffink terribibble has happened to me! Mum says she didn't need to fink those forts, and now she's feeling skin-crawly and sick. And remembering all the gentle kisses I've gived her over the past couple of days.

June 30

I metted a new friend at the beach today. His name is Charlie and he's a little black shaggy fella who lives with his Mum, Erica. Charlie is the most himportant soul in Erica's life. She losted her husband, Al, this year. Al had somefing called Parkinsons Disease as well as Vascular Dementia, but Charlie didn't notice this a-very-tall. He used to lie with Al when he was feeling poorly-sick, and give Erica somefing else to very fink about and horganise. Charlie and Erica are getting used to the world without Al which, for Erica, after fifty years of being with Al, is a lot of getting used to. And it's Charlie's himportant work to do helping with this.

Charlie has decided that the bestest way to help is to collect every single actual ball in Suffolk. And then not do giving them back. On a beach in June, there be a very lot of balls. Trying to explain to Charlie that they is not all *his* balls is hard actual work, hespecially for me because I do not really hunderstand wot balls are for. You can chuck one about and I will watch you go and collect it if that makes you happy, but I aren't going to be doing that for you, no matter how many times you ask.

I decided to do helping Erica with Charlie-the-ball-thief by trying to distract him, and encourage him to play so that Erica could grab the stolen ball and return it to the peoples wot he had nicked it from. I had to do this very, very quite a lot and quickerly, because although Charlie is not speedy at running, he is super-sneakery at looking like he is playing with you whilst keeping a quite very beady eye on his balls. Well, not *his* balls. Everyboddedy else's balls wot he is not planning on giving back. The concept of sharing is completely losted on Charlie, but he is a fabumazing companion for Erica, and she meets lots of new peoples when she is with Charlie. Mostly cos she's saying sorry-about-the-ball-fing. Maybe this is Charlie's cunning plan for helping his Mum make new friends, and do getting used to life without Al.

Mum says that when the previously ginger one was really, wheely unwell last year, I did give Mum lots to fink about apart from worrying about whether the previously ginger one was going to get betterer, and wondering if the poxy guv'ment had any idea how stoopid it was putting a poorly-sick child in a Opital 200 miles from her famberly. I did lots of distracting her and making her smile without realising it. I also did a very lot of eating Kindles, which is very actual similar to Charlie's ball-stealing game. Us doggies will always find a way of making fings betterer, even if it do not seem so at the time.

JULY

July 1

Frank is the fugest cat I has ever met. He is tall and he is quite actual fat, and he has the longest tail I has ever, hever seen. But for some actual reason he decided tonight that he wasn't fuge and fat, and he was a ickle little kitten that could very definitely, easily fit into the cardboard box Dad had left on the kitchen table.

And it's quite actual true, he *could* fit into it. He jammed himself into it and wented to sleep, but I fink whilst he was asleep he must have dunned growing some more cos, when he tried to get out, he couldn't! So he struggled a little bit and that maded the box fall over. And then when he *still* couldn't get out, he managed to claw onto the side of the table and tip himself and the box onto the floor, with the box hupside down and Frank still inside it.

Most cats in Frank's predickerment would dunned Complaints to the Management, and perhaps asked for some actual help getting out of the redickerless situation. But not Frank. Frank just decided he'd go back to sleep again. When Dad camed into the kitchen to make a cuppatea, he did notice the box was on the floor, but assumed me and Gandhi had been bopping fings about the place. And anyway, he was more actual hinterested in muttering about the larder door being lefted open *again*, and did we want even more mouses in the house than last year?

Dad carried on his muttering and moaning about the larder door, and was he the honly person who ever shutted it, and it wasn't until he was carrying three cuppateas that he did even notice the box. Cos he kicked it by haccident. In his head, the box was empty and light, and was supposed to skitterer across the floor, and not cause any problems. Hinstead, it was like kicking a brick. Dad stopped, and all of a very actual sudden ... and I aren't sure wot happened next cos I did running away bravely when the tea started sloppering everywhere, and the words beginning with B begunned flying about.

As Dad isn't in very general a yeller or a words-beginning-with-B-roarer kind of chap, Mum camed running. And founded Dad kneeling in a fuge puddle of tea, trying to rip the cardboard box to bits to release Frank, and make sure he wasn't drowning in the tea that was everywhere.

Mum decided not to do laughing at Dad and his soggy trousers, and the quite very hoffended but fortunately not actual drowned Frank and stucked the kettle on again. And mopped up the floor. But mainly, very quietly, maded sure the larder door was shut.

July 6

Today, we is all wondering wot the world has comed to and if we need to do some serious re-finking. Mouse – our Mouse, the one who can't

remember how to use the stairs, and who has wonned every award for
'Cat least likely' ever hinvented – caughted a mouse. And carried it into
the house alive and wriggerling, so we is pretty sure she didn't just find
it. It's quite very actual hard to just find a live mouse in the garden, I do
reckon. To be actual honest, I wouldn't have ever, hever fort Mouse was
capable of finding even a dead one.

Mouse was as useless at deading the mouse as every other cat
in this house, except for Gandhi, so me and my famberly spent the rest
of the evening trying to catch the mouse and heject it from the house
before it tooked up residence in the larder. I fink I was helpful. Well, I did
wot everyboddedy else was doing, which was aimlessly running around,
peering under the fridge and joining in with barking hinstructions to
no-one in particular. I was a very quite actual exerlent team player in that
respect, though I'm not sure that any of us was quite actual playing on the
same team.

Or even in the same game, and very quite actual not with the same
rules.

After Dad bended his knee wrong and had to be dragged out from
under the fridge, and Mum gave up trying to catch the mouse and just
stood in the middle of the kitchen flapping and saying rude fings about
mouses, kitchens, cats, and mainly Dads who can't follow hinstructions,
the previously ginger one decided that catching mouses is not a team
game but a so-low sport, and tolded us all to go away and carrying on
woofing, and flapping and not being able to walk somewhere else.

They was still harguing about mouses, and wondering if Dad
needed a noo knee, and how someboddedy has to be the team leader
and why is it always Mum, when the previously ginger one tried to sneak
past the hoffice and up the stairs with the ickle, dorable, soon-to-become-
Pet-Mouse in a box.

'No!' shoutered Mum and Dad at hexactly the same time. They
might be actual rubbish at being a Team when it comes to catching
mouses. But they is epic at it when it comes to being parents. The
previously ginger one is sulking very big time badly now; the mouse is
running around in the field, and Mouse the cat is back sitting at the top of
the stairs wondering how to get down.

July 8

Today I are wondering if I has missed the point about pebbles.

Pip is completely hobsessed with pebbles, and I is wondering
wot she finks they are and who she finks she actual is. If she sees a good
pebble on our walk she will shout at it, and run around it, then shout at
her Mum and digger around it, and then try to bury it, and then digger it
up again. And I does not know why she is so hexcited about them.

I used to fink maybe Pip fort she was a chicken and the pebble was
a negg. That would make sense of why she is hobsessed with diggering
them out and do not want to leave them alone. But she doesn't make a
nest and sit on it. And she's never tried to bring one home. She wouldn't

be so stoopid as to try and eat it, and rarely does trying to carry one in her mouth.

She might fink they is a ball because if her Mum sees a Pip-shaped pebble she will sometimes gently roll it along the ground so that Pip can notice it, and then do her burying and diggering and shoutering game with it. But if you pick it up and roll it again, she isn't that actual hinterested, she's too busy looking for another one, and to be actual quite honest, by the time Pip has finished doing her fing with the pebble, she is usually miles and miles behind the rest of us. Has you ever tried to find the same pebble on a walk? I don't fink the hoomans have good enuff noses for that sort of fing, and Pip's usually buried the pebble so noboddedy could find it hanyway.

My bestest guess is that Pip finks the pebbles be treasure. And Pip is a very quite forgetful pirate. She buries the treasure and then has to digger it up to check it's still where she lefted it. And then gets all hexcited and barky about finding it again cos she's forgotted she buried it honly thirty seconds ago. And then when she hears her Mum calling her, she forgets to remember to bury it again because she's more concentrating on not letting herself get too far behind.

Being Pip-the-forgetful-pirate must be quite very actual hard work. For a start, there's so many pebbles on our walk, she must wonder how she's ever going to actual bury them all! And once she's buried them, I has no hidea how she's going to do remembering which ones is treasure and which ones is just, well, pebbles wot have gotted buried by the farmer. And I can't see how she's planning to keep her treasures a secret so they don't get stealed, cos she shouts so much about the pebbles, hoomans in Norfolk can hear her. And everywhere she walks, there is a little pile of mud and scrabbling wot says 'Pip's treasure is very HERE.' It's like 'X marks the spot' on a map, except X is the spot and there's no map. It's just hobvious on the ground.

Sometimes, I fink I would like to *be* Pip. She's ickle so she gets exerlent cuddles and snuggles on hoomans' laps. She's quite spritely so she can jump onto beds no problem a-very-tall. And she is so bossy and Sertive, everyboddedy does wot she actual wants, just for some actual peace and quiet.

And then I do remember the forgetful pirate stuff and I are quite actual glad I are Worzel Wooface, who don't need no treasure, and very quite actual definitely does not want to be a forgetful pirate.

No fank oo.

July 9

Mum's binned fishally told her shoulder is betterer and she doesn't need to be squashed any more. She still has to do wiggling it around at home and pushing it up against a wall whenever she remembers. Sometimes, I do walk past Mum and wonder wot on very earth she is doing, and then she makes grunty noises like a sheep trying to push a lamb out of its boddedy and I remember. The fizzy-o-ferapy man says if she keeps going with the grunting and the lamb pushing, it'll keep getting betterer now quite quickerly. Mum is actual happy about this.

July 11

I've honly binned offered I Scream once. It was in the Limpic Park last year when it was very actual hot, and I had binned an exerlent boykin doing sailing and going on trains and not having hystericals about anyfing. But I didn't like it. I fort it was scaredy stuff and refused to do eating it. Mum says this was very actual odd after all the fings I did not hobject to, but seeing as I Scream is not a very hessential part of my diet, she hasn't dunned offering it to me again.

But if I did like I Scream, I could have it every day. Every. Single. Blinking. Day according to Dad, and he doesn't know how peoples with small children in our village cope cos the I Scream van man has decided to come down our lane every day so far this month. And if he hears the out-of-tune-tinny-country-dance-music one more time he's going to scream. Or be doing a Manly Yell, he means. Not scream. Screaming is for girls. And little boys. And their poor Mums, we all fink, who must be sick by now of being naggered about the I Scream van.

Even though the hoomans in our village quite like I Scream, they is refusing to do buying some from the man now in case it hencourages him to keep on coming round. Whenever Mum or Dad hear the I Scream van, they has taken to either shoutering rude fings, or if they is in the garden, stomping indoors and banging the door shut.

And I has taken to joining in with a lot of barking and a teeny-tiny bit of chasing Frank through the cat-flap, which is very not acceptababble.

I are blaming the I Scream Van Man but Mum says it's her fault for shoutering and slamming doors whenever she hears him coming. She's taughted me to react to it.

Now Dad's looking on Uff the Confuser to find out about ASBOs for I Scream vans, and Mum's wondering why I refuse to do learning about a clicker but are quite happy to bark and chase when I hear country dance music.

July 12

When Dad went to work today, Mum gotted out her recorder to see if I would do barking at the same music played in tune and without the moaning and the door-slamming. I just looked at her and worried about the stick fing she was blowing down. So I did runaway and hide at the top of the landing till she putted it away.

Mum's feeling slightly stoopid now and has decided not to tell Dad.

July 13

Today, I will be hiding in the house from the big green giant saucer fing in the garden. Wot is full of water from the scaredy, spitting, yellow snake. Until I do remembering that it's my paddling pool and wot it is actual for. Then I will be causing chaos.

Worzel Wooface

July 14

Last night, the food delivery man did arrive and he was very quite late. Usually, I do like to let delivery men fink I are much more himpressive than I are, because there is somefing about a man carrying several fuge green boxes that is quite actual scary and they do deserve to be shoutered at.

The man last night was hot and late, and his van had broked down, so he was quite very fed up. Mum did decide that the best place for me was out of the way in the hall, but then Dad decided he would help with the puttering away (which had Mum wondering if he was poorly-sick), and I did use this hopportunity to wriggle through to hintroduce myself to the man.

Mum quickerly asked if the man "was okay with dogs?" as she spectacully failed to grab my collar as I wriggled past her, and was already doing "pleased-to-meet-you-BOY-you-is-sticky-hot-lemme-lick-you" hellos.

"I'm fine with dogs," the man said, and his voice went all squashed and full of air and flat, and I definitely gotted the himpression that dogs were the honly fing he was actual fine with at that moment.

I suddenly noticed that under the aroma of sitting-in-a-hot-van-waiting-for-someone-to-rescue-him was a dog biscuit. In the man's pocket. Wot he was not getting out to offer to Worzel Wooface. So I did do plitely reminding him that he was in my kitchen, and could he do handing it over. Please-and-fanking-oo-kindly.

"Sit," he said.

For a second I did fink of declining his offer, seeing as how he was in *my* kitchen and I hadn't doned scaring the living wotsits out of him. But then I did look at him and forted he needed somefing, ANYFING to go actual very right that day.

So I did sit. And he did hand over the biscuit.

Mum's eyebrows did disappear off her face. She saided several fings like 'flipping 'eck, Worzel you blinking fraud.' She tolded the man he was Onored and other fings ilke that to make sure he hunderstood how hunusual and generous me doing sit for a complete stranger was, and he wented back to his van with a spring in his step.

Well, he would've dunned if he hadn't been carrying eight Tesco boxes wot were making his trousers try to fall down his legs. I hope he did happreciate my good deed of the day. I quite very actual happreciated his biscuit and I has decided that this delivery man can come again. Mum actual hagrees with me, although she'd rather that next time he isn't three hours late, and do not be drippering quite so much sweat onto the floor.

July 15

Mum's all hexcited this morning. Her pear tree has got four ickle pears on it. I do fink her appiness is very quite strange. Dad keeps reminding Mum that once-a-very-pon-a-time, we had an ickle napple tree that was dorable and had four ickle napples on it. And now we has a monster-triffid-over-very-fusey-tastic napple tree that is very quite causing chaos,

80

continued page 89

Snow is fabumazing once it has stopped moving. Before that, it is quite very actual horrid.

I are very quite glad that Mum and Louise has stopped wearing a moustache and waving sticks around. So is Dad. (Courtesy Nick Butcher, Lowestoft Journal)

The quite very actual smelly suprise Mum collected from Milton Keynes. She tooked this photo at the start of the journey. By the end, fings were not quite so clean ...

Trying to get Hazel to go in the puddles was himpossible.

The front end of Hazel sort of looked like a dog. The back end did quite very not ...

Lying in the sun with the front door open is wonder-veryful. Even if Mum does get a bit chilly when we do ask to do this in March.

Hazel fort she could get on this bed. Hazel is very oppy-mistic, I do fink.

My perfick birthday was always going to hinvolve mud.

My Dad is fabumazing and did decide to show me how to play with Oink the Piggywiggy.

We does live near a beach, wot I are very quite glad about, as playing there with my Dad after work is great very fun!

(All images courtesy Kerry Jordan)

Toy-playing with Hazel. We did both learn to take turns and play nicely.

I does not want to be discussing how much I hated wearing a buster collar but I will never, hever be wearing one again.

Gipsy-was-Pandy the foster fridge. She is now the same size as a caravan.

No matter wot I do, Hazel Will. Not. get her feets wet!

Playing in the watermeadow with Nelson. If I lie down we get as wet as each actual other.

Lola meets the gang.

Pirate Pip with one of her treasure pebbles

When I play with Mattie it is always very quite hard to find the front bit under all that hair. (Courtesy Kerry Jordan)

Mum says I are not allowed to squash bluebells when she is trying to take hartistic pictures of me ... heven if they has fox poo hunderneath them.

and Mum fuge amounts of work and troubles every summer. "The definition of madness is doing the same thing again and again and hoping the outcome will be different," Dad do say.

But pears, Mum says, is not napples, and Dad has got no actual answer to that.

Apart from running away down to the boat and hiding. I aren't sure if he's hiding from Mum or the fruit trees.

Probababbly both ...

July 16

Dad's binned a very quite actual naughty boy. And Mum's hero. He can do breaking into cars wot I shouldn't probababbly tell you, but he says it should be okay as long as I tell you he can honly if he actual has to. And he actual had to cos Mum is a blithering hidiot. I aren't allowed to tell you how he didded it, though. The main fing is that Mum's stopped having hystericals about me gettering locked in the car, and stopped finking about breaking all the windows. And I've stopped jumping around on the back seat watching Dad doing his criminal hactivity, setting off the car alarm and waking up all the neighbours.

July 19

Mum says she can cope with the baby bunnies. She can cope with the endless mice-trafficking. She heventually got over the squirrel lefted on top of the kettle like some terribibble warning from a scaredy film, but none of us is actual very speaking to Gipsy-the-Cat today. She broughted in a still-alive Goldfinch wot had to be tooked to Boris-the-Vet to be putted out of its suffering. Catching birds is bad enuff. Catching birds and then bringing them into the house means you is in the Doghouse. Or, in the case of Gipsy, you get chucked out and the cat-flap locked until Mum can do forgiving you.

July 20

I are really sad tonight. My good friend Ghost has died. It was very sudden so we is all very actual shocked as well. I hope you do remember that Ghost was the very first growed-up boykin dog I did meet. Because he was a big boykin dog wot did not put up with hidiotic babies like I used to be, Mum trusted Ghost and his Mum, Claire, to teach me doggy manners and how to be respectful.

Ghost was also super-fast and clever. He was the first dog who worked out how to catch me by cutting off corners. When he did this he would nip my bum so I knowed he had won. The first time he did it, I did nearly actual fall over because I was so shocked and surprised.

Ghost had a fuge deep bark wot was frilling HAND scaredy, and when he did chasing me I always fort I was in a proper game. All our forts and finking is with Claire, Paul, Robyn and Beth tonight. Ghost will always be remembered with love.

July 21

Dear Gypsy-the-Fridge

I hears you have hadded your hoperation to stop you being a stroppy Diva and gettering preggerant. According to your Dad all of actual Lincolnshire did hear you howling about it, and the vet-man was quite actual glad when your Dad camed to pick you up.

So was the cat wot was having to be in the same room as you.

I are very quite himpressed you did finking of howling and yelling to get out of that actual place. I are rubbish at that kind of fing and have to do epic sulking and looking sorry for myself if I are somewhere I does not want to be. Or do chewing through my lead. But I fink vets are quite cunning and clever and do not do falling for that ol' trick.

I hope you does feel better very actual soon, and you does not have to do wearing a hateful buster collar. But remember my cunning plan wot I mentioned before: if you do see one, sit on it. I are very quite sure you will be able to do that fing because any dog wot can break the vet's scales by being too big, and not being able to get all their feets and their bum on the scales at the same time should be able to squash a buster collar, no problem a-very-tall.

From your luffly boykin

Worzel Wooface

July 24

Gipsy-the-Cat has gotted another blinking chest hinfection. She seems to get them a quite very lot, which is worrying Mum and Dad. Boris-the-Vet gived her two hinjections, HAND stucked his fermometer up her bum. Gipsy must be feeling quite very poorly because she did not do objectoring to this fing. She didn't even pee all over the table like she does normally actual do.

Boris-the-Vet reckons we have caughted it, so she should perk up quite quickerly and I will not be having to be Nurse Wooface like last time. I are quite actual glad about this because if Gipsy hasn't dunned Complaints to the Management about the needle-sticking and bum-hinvading, she is going to feel the need to take it out on someboddedy very quite actual soon. I are going to be steering clear ...

July 25

Auntie Sue and Uncle Dave drove all the way from Corny Wall to see me for half-an-hour today. I are a very special Worzel Wooface, I know, but driving sixteen hours to see me for half-an-hour is a bit actual hexcessive, I do fink. I probababbly would have been okay without the visit but it was quite very actual kind of them. They tried to do pretendering they was delivering a tent to someboddedy close to where I do live, but they didn't very actual fool me. I know they camed to see the luffly boykin, Worzel Wooface.

I are a bit worried now, though. Dad promised me that all the mad peoples are on Mum's side of the famberly. I fink he has been fibbering about this, though, and now I is wondering wot else he has been fibbering about ...

TWO INTO ONE WON'T GO

Putting a cat in a travelling
crate
To take her to the vet
Should not be too difficult
And lead to fights, and yet

It's probably much easier
And won't cause vessels to
burst
In your head, if you do check
Frank's not got in there first

I left the kitchen very fast
When all the hissing began
And when mum sawed wot she
had done.
She followed at a run

Mum's trying to find the
telephone
To give the vet a call
She can't bring Gipsy in today
She's bouncing off the walls

July 27

Something very actual hexciting and himportant is happening today. I are going to Lola's house for my very first ever sleepover. I has never dunned sleeping in someboddedy else's house before, so this is all noo and different. This will be a Trial Run for when my famberly go on a hollibob.

Mum and Dad and the previously ginger one are going to go to Holland on the boat in a few weeks' time. Ever since Dad did get permoted in January, he can't just do bogging off when he quite very actual feels like it. He has to be responsibabble, which Mum says is a whole new hexperience for him. So they has to be horganised and do coming back so that other actual peoples can go on their hollibobs as well.

Which means that I can't go. You might be finking that is odd because I aren't responsibabble for anyfing other than being a luffly boykin, but you has to hunderstand about the sea.

The sea can do all kinds of very strange fings. It can be all lumpy and windy and not very nice one day. And then smooth and perfick but with no wind on another day, so you end up floating around going nowehere a-very-tall forever. Me and Mum fink it is fabumazing when it is hot and the wind is hardly moving, and we get to do sun-worshipping and Mum gets to do wobbling around the deck wearing nuffink but suntan cream. But Dad doesn't. Not the Mum wearing nuffink bit: he says he's not prepared to answer that cos wotever he says will land him in the Doghouse. But when we has to have a hollibob between two fixed actual dates cos someboddedy else needs to get on a plane to go to Spain, me being on the boat isn't a good idea. Cos if it is too lumpy and windy, Mum will have hystericals and say it is too blinking rough for Worzel Wooface and we can't leave yet. And the man going to Spain will be hupset when he misses his plane, and it will all be a disasterer.

Mum can just about very cope with sailing across the sea, even if it is a bit rough, so long as she can do moaning about it and threaten Dad with all kinds of gardening jobs when they get back. But not if Worzel Wooface is on board. That would be too very actual much. And coming back is even more complercated cos I aren't allowed to come back across the sea in our boat, even though I wented on it, but have to go on somefing called a Fairy Boat because of the 'poxy guv'ment.' A Fairy Boat wot you has to book months in advance if you wants to bring back a dog, which do mean we could end up with the Fairy Boat booked before we've even been able to leave if the weather is bad, and I are very going on the trip. Dogs and boats togetherer is not all that actual easy.

So, instead of me going for a sailing trip, I are going to stay with John and Jill, who be Lola's Mum and Dad. Everyboddedy finks this is a fabumazing idea cos Jill is as hobsessed about wot's-best-for-her-dogs as Mum is.

Dad says I will have a luffly time at my Trial Run, and I are a lucky boykin cos Jill and John, Lola's Mum and Dad, are really, wheely looking forward to it. And he's not fibbering about this fing. He's hoping like actual mad it all goes well, cos otherwise fings will be quite very himpossible with the hollibob and his sailing, wot is halmost as himportant to him as I are. He says he's not fibbering about that fing, either. Well, maybe a little bit. In the end, we settled for both as himportant as each other, but he gets to see me every day and really honly gets to go sailing a couple of times a year. And could I not do cocking it up for him. Please.

Mum has been wailing about whether I will do behaving myself, and whether she has taughted me everyfing I are supposed to know. Dad says Jill doesn't need three pages of hinstructions, especially as she only lives a mile down the road and can use a telephone perfectly well.

Mum's not sure; she says it's almost as bad as the fuge ginger boyman's first day at school but with less chance of me peeing on the floor.

July 28

I are back from my sleepover and I did mainly like it. Apart from the sleeping-over bit. I liked the playing and the being made a fuss of, and I loved the pottering round the garden having a quiet time with John, and I definitely liked the rampaging around and almost-but-not-quite-completely-trashing Jill's flower beds.

But then it got to the bit where I was supposed to go to bed in my own house with my own toys, and most actual very himportantly with MY OWN MUM ... and it didn't happen. So I spended most of the night wandering about lookering for her and wondering when she was actual coming back, and slightly-a-bit-quite-a-lot-really noisy disturbering stuff like that.

Fings gotted betterer after breakfast (wot I did decided to eat cos I was a bit famished from all the lookering and waiting for Mum all night) cos I sawed Dad. He was quite very actual pleased to see me but a bit concerned about me being Up. All. Night. Dad says when he did sleeping over at people's houses when 'ewasaboy' he did staying up all night and being naughty. Then he said as he was now a proper grown-up he had to go and do some work and I had to do Managing in the Hoffice. To be actual quite honest, I did whining and moaning in the Hoffice but happarently lots of peoples do that, too, so that wasn't unbearababble.

When I gotted home, I did go and find Mum and just stooded there Staring. At. Her. for a long time. I did not do going bonkers-crazy-pleased-to-see-you because ... well, I don't know why I did not but once I did find Mum everyfing was very okay again. So, now I are sleeping off my sleepover in my own house.

Jill and Mum fink it would be a good idea if I did have another Trial Run next week to see if I are more settled. I'm not actual quite very sure that this will be okay. But I are two now, and Mum says I has got to have another try at this being-a-big-boy stuff.

July 30

Mum just haccidentally flea-treated Dad. Cos I don't like my neck being fiddled around with, Mum uses somefing called Billy-No-Mates in my dinner, wot is a mixture of herby fings. It makes my food taste a bit like flowers but it's better than the dreaded drops, and 24 hours of me having a big fat sulk (she says). And it works very quite actual well.

I aren't sure Dad needed to be flea-treated but when Mum was making him a dinner of Spaghetti BogNog she haccidentally grabbed the wrong pot. She was tidying up in the kitchen later and sawed the wrong pot next to the cooker.

She's had a look at the hingredients wot do go in my dinner, and they are all actual fings wot you could feed a hooman, so she says everyfing is going to be fine, so long as Dad isn't preggerant. And so long as he doesn't find out wot happened ...

July 31

Last night, we tried that sleeping-over fing again, but this time we tooked my old crate along to see if that did do helping. It did! It did do helping a quite very actual lot.

There was a moment when I did find someboddedy's shoes to

play with, but that wasn't my fault, happarently, and there was talk about people's learning to put them away like they've binned told a billion times before. When I gotted home I did not do giving Mum or Dad any of those hard stares like wot doggies do when they is hoffended, but I did waggy-tail-wotcha-Mum-why's-Dad-still-in-bed-hellos, so we is all set and ready for the hollibob, and I are very quite actual pleased with myself, and so is Mum.

Visit Hubble and Hattie on the web: www.hubbleandhattie.com
www.hubbleandhattie.blogspot.co.uk • Details of all books • Special offers
• Newsletter • New book news

AUGUST

August 1

Mum and Dad say that having a night off from me lummoxing about on top of them was marvellous. Apart from NOT having me lummoxing about on top of them. Hoomans are very strange like this and I do not hunderstand how they can fink two fings at the same time. It's called mixed forts, apparently, and it's somefing hoomans can do but I don't fink dogs can. I fink one fing at a time. Wot I are finking about right now is how to convince Mum and Dad that they need to be finking more about how weird and odd it was without me on the bed, and how reassuring it is to know I are there between them, and less on how marvellous it was not to wake up with pins and needles, or a Worzel foot in their mouth. Otherwise, they might start finking about shuttering the bedroom door with me on the wrong side of it again. Wot I DO NOT want to happen.

August 2

After the hooman mixed forts of yesterday, I did fink it would be a quite very actual good idea if I did working out wot I fort about beds. So that I can do communercating it to the hoomans.

****FORTS ON BEDS****

- 🛏 I know I has my own personal bed. And I luffs it. But it is for the daytime, not the night-time.
- 🛏 I do not be wanting to come under the duvet. Even if you is freezing. I are not a Whippet. Also you has elbows under there.
- 🛏 If you get out of bed to go to the loo, I will always be lying on the warm bit you just left. Please could you stop sittering on me when you come back. We've been doing this for over a year now.
- 🛏 If Dad is snoring and Mum shouts at him, I will assume Mum is shoutering at me and jump off the bed. Then I will wait until she has finally nearly got over Dad's snoring, and has nearly actual finally falled asleep at last, and choose this moment to leap back onto the bed and wake her up again.
- 🛏 Me shakering and wobbling my feet when I are asleep is called dreaming. Not me having a fit. Please stop waking me up.
- 🛏 It is definitely Dad who needs his toenails clippering before he rips any more holes in the duvet with his feets. Not me.
- 🛏 It is definitely Mum who leaves crumbs in the bed. Not me.
- 🛏 Trying to convince me that there is more room on the previously ginger one's bed would work betterer if she didn't share it with three cats.
- 🛏 We needs a biggerer bed.

I fink number actual ten is the himportant one I do need to communercate to Mum and Dad. Most of the other 'issues' would be solved it we did this fing. Apart from the toenails and the crumbs, but Mum and Dad are currently grumbling to each other about these fings and it hasn't occurred to them it might be me. In which case I shall mainly be keeping very actual quiet about them fings.

August 3

Dad says there aren't room for a biggerer bed. We already has the fugest bed that will fit in the room. He also says blaming him for having ripping-duvet-toenails would work betterer if I remembered that his feets always stay down the bottom of the bed, unlike mine wot leap around all over the blinking place. And unless he's got duvet-ripping-teeth – wot he says he very actual quite hasn't – the holes are down to me. But the crumbs is Mum. Definitely Mum and her blinking bags of crisps wot she eats in bed.

To be actual quite honest, they could be a little bit my fault. You see, sometimes when Mum is having a sneaky midday power nap, she will take a bag of crisps upstairs to eat before she has a snooze. And every time she has crisps, she does offer me one. And I do hignore them. Hunlike Mum, I do not want to eat crisps in bed. So I leave them, and Mum actual forgets about them and then I squash them. And that's how we get crumbs in the bed.

I fink if Dad did know this he would get even crosser about the crumbs in the bed cos he would wonder why it is so himportant that I have to like crisps in the bed as much as Mum does. And could she work on our bonding-over-crisps stuff somewhere else. *Anywhere* else.

August 4

Someboddedy better have a word with this summer fing cos since it wented missing I has binned getting into all sorts of very actual troubles.

The last few days all it has doned here is Rain. And winded. Lots of wind wot has been quite actual scary at times. It has definitely not been luffly-boykin-Sighthound weather. We hasn't been able to go for a walk ALL weekend. So when Mum and the previously ginger one wented to the cinema last night and I had a teeny-weeny chew on a not-very-himportant cushion on Mum's bed, Dad said I was forgived as it was hunderstandable I was bored.

I was less forgived when I refused to go out into the garden after my dinner. And waited until Dad was in the bath to do a poo in the hall. This is totally hunacceptable for a boy-who-is-two-wot-had-been-offered-outside-just-before-Dad-did-getting-in-the-bath, and especially as Dad was still in the bath when Mum gotted home from the cinema. She founded the poo and tolded off Dad for being useless, wot he actual very wasn't, but Mum wasn't hinterested in his hexcuses.

I wented outside this morning but only because Mabel-the-mad-cat was completely soaking wet on the back doorstep. For reasons known honly to Mabel, the cat-flap is currently Not. In. Service. It's working perfectly actual very well for all the other cats, but in Mabel's head it's becomed the Tunnel of Doom and she won't go through it. SO, when I sawed a very windswept Mabel on the doorstep I did leapering and woofing out of the door, then chased her up the napple tree. Chasing Mabel is NUMBER ONE on the list of fings Worzel Wooface must very actual quite NOT EVER, HEVER DO.

Mum has finally managed to persuade Mabel that living in the napple tree isn't a long-term hoption, mainly because the wind blew and napples started bouncing off the tree like bullets. So now I'm in the Doghouse, Mabel is planning to hassassinate me, and Mum's gotted a sore head.

Come rain or shine, we're going out this afternoon.

August 6

Did you know that frowing bits of vegetababbles against a wall is very actual ferapootic Mum recommends it. It doesn't make a mess, it's very quiet, so noboddedy has a art attack, and it kind of bounces so you can pick it up and do it again. And very again. If it doesn't bounce back and you are Really. Fed. Up. Dad will pick up the bits and hand them back to you until you remember that you are a grown-up.

It's very actual quite definitely not my fault. It was a haccident, but next time, happarently, I are to do actual Limping or Not. Eating. or SOMEFING cos Mum isn't telly-pafic. In future, if I has cutted the hinside of my thigh, could I not act like there is nuffink wrong and belt around a water meadow for forty-five minutes, then come home and eat my dinner, and generally be completely actual normal and not bleed anywhere and finally decide to show Mum the next day?

Cos now I has got to have manuka honey and antibiotics and road walks and boring stuff like that. To be actual very honest, I woulda had to have all that boring stuff hanyway, it's just that Mum wouldn't have felt like such a hidiot.

Which is why Mum knows that frowing bits of vegetababbles at a wall can be helpful in certain situations.

But the worstest fing of all is that Mum is refusing quite very actual point-blank to go on hollibob until my leg is better, and they was supposed to be leaving at the weekend. She'll worry too actual much about my leg, she says, and I can't go and be on bed-rest with Lola, Sam and Sim cos it won't be bed rest, it'll be super-dooper-bitey-facey zoomies, and she's not hinflicting that kind of chaos on Jill and John. Dad has binned very actual quite simperfetic and hunderstanding, but is also actual very, very hupset. It looks like their hollibob has just gotted cancelled ...

August 7

Sometimes, Mum is so busy being my Mum, and the previously ginger's Mum, and fuge ginger boyman's Mum that she forgets a quite very actual himportant fing. Which is that she's got her *own* Mum who I do call the

Dog-Hexpert, cos, well, she is: the most Doggiest-Hexpert in the world apart from me. And I are honly betterer at being a Dog-Hexpert than her cos I are a actual dog. The Dog-Hexpert is the one person who can get away with telling Mum wot to do and absolutely flipping hinsistering that Dad and the rest of the hoomans need a hollibob. And Mum WILL be going away at the weekend, and that's the very end of it.

Now, I know it is my very actual leg wot has caused all this kerfuffle, and me not bothering to let anyboddedy know I had a big ol' cut on my thigh so it couldn't be fixed all quick, but I do fink I is being very quite hard dunned by. I've got to go and actual stay with Dog-Hexpert. On my actual very own. Without Mum there to say that I don't have to do sit, and that I aren't cut out for Working Trials. She's heven going to do putting the cream on my leg wot makes me wobble when Mum actual does it.

I has decided that I has got no choice but to do wot I is tolded about this fing; partly cos me jumpering into a gorse bush and being a plonker and not telling anyboddedy I was hurted caused the problem in the first place, but mainly cos the Dog-Hexpert says so, and noboddedy argues with her. Not. Even. Mum.

August 9

Tomorrow I are going to stay with the Dog-Hexpert. Everyfing is going to be actual fine (we has binned told). Mum has also binned hinformed that there is no need for me to do having sleepovers to check I are alright and well behaved. I will be well behaved, and even if I are actual not, Mum will be in the middle of the North Sea tomorrow, and won't be able for do anyfing about it.

The Dog-Hexpert has this way of saying stuff that you just have to do agreeing with. Dad is hoping I are as good as doing wot I are told as all the hoomans in the Dog-Hexpert's life. When Dad did say this to the Dog-Hexpert, she did Give. Him. A. Look. It's the same look Mum gives Dad but it's had 25 more years hexperience. He shutted up. And went down to finish sorting out the boat for the hollibob tomorrow before he disolved into a pile of wet and wobbly man, wot isn't capable of doing steering the boat.

August 11

Dear Famberly,

I hope you is having a fabumazing hollibob. From wot the Dog-Hexpert has tolded me, the crossing was perfick to start off with and then gotted very windy and lumpy. I are glad I wasn't actual on board.

Fings has binned very quite hinteresting here. I has surprised my actual self with the fings I has agreed to do. I has learned to do 'over' and also 'through.'

'Over' is a thirty centipeder little fence fing wot I have to do jumping over to get to my sleepering place. It has a hinside and a houtside bit. 'Through' is to get to the houtside bit for some fresh air or if I do need weesandpoos during the night. It's a very small 'through' but

Gran gotted Baillie, her clever Collie, to show me how to actual do it. After that, the Dog-Hexpert did her 'you-will-be-keen-to-do-wot-I-ask' magic and I worked out how to wriggle and squiggle through, heven though I fort I might be too fuge. Gran-the-Dog-Hexpert said much bigger dogs have gotted through it and I was to get on with it. I gotted on with it.

You might be wondering wot I fink of this kennel fing but, trust me, it's far, far betterer than in the actual house. For a start it is quiet and safe, and most himportant of all, nowhere near Baillie who is bonkers-crazy.

I dunno wot Gran feeds Baillie but wotever it is, she needs to stop. Or tell somebodddey himportant that she has discovered the Fountain of Youth. Baillie is twelve and finks he is six months old. He can bounce for Ingerland. All he does is bounce and do tricks and try to horganise everyboddedy, and then bounce some more and then do a cuddle trick and ... it goes on and on.

And on. All day. Every day. If you just look at him, he does somefing clever.

Fortunately, I are not hexpected to be clever. It is very overrated and quite actual hexhausting.

August 13
Dear Dad

I has got some bad news. I fink Mum and the Dog-Hexpert share quite a very lot of jeans. Gran-the-Dog-Hexpert and Mum both wave their hands about when they is hexcited. They also like eating vegetababbles and horrid stuff like that.

Mum and the Dog-Hexpert say lots of fings the same. Like 'Don't Be So Redickerless.' I has binned called redickerless for all kinds of perfickly not redickerless fings over the past few days.

Being scared of Iona is not redickerless I do fink, even though she looks like a cute and dorable Cavalier King Charles Spaniel. Refusing to go through a back door in case Iona eats me is also not redickerless. Once Gran-the-Dog-Hexpert did pick up Iona from around my ankles to stop her being a shrieking banshee, I did decide it was okay to go through the door. There is some fings a luffly boykin will Not Do, even for the Dog-Hexpert's magic, and walk through a door Iona is guarding is one of them fings. Gran-the-Dog-Hexpert says Iona is all-mouth-and-no-trousers which is all quite very well, but it's the mouth bit I are worried about.

So, wot with the vegetababble-eating and the hand-waving and the 'Don't be so redickerlesses,' I are certain they has got lots of the same jeans, which means that Mum might get heven more like the Dog-Hexpert when she is olderer. I are sure you can't have actual knowed this when you did getting married to Mum. I fink our house is going to get bossier. And messier. Sorry if this is a shock.

August 15
Dear previously ginger one

I fink you do share jeans with Mum and the Dog-Hexpert. I fink you should stop eating vegetababbles very actual now or you'll end up like them when you is finished growing up.

August 17
Dear Gipsy-the-Cat

You would be very actual quite proud of me today. I has binned doing my bestest best manners and following some hinstructions wot I did learn from you and from bitter hexperience. According to Gran, that makes me a 'blessed relief.' Wot sounds very himpressive.

I has binned using the very-himportant-pretend-Gipsy-do-not-hexist-and-be-a-respectful-boykin lessons you teached me with a dog called Roxy. Roxy has special knees, happarently. I couldn't see anyfing wrong with her knees a-very-tall but there is definitely somefing wrong in her head. Gran says I are not to take it personally; she is like that with everyboddedy. I did exerlent hignoring of Roxy and Gran was very pleased with me about that.

August 19
Dear Mum

I has completely forgotted to tell you how fabumazing I has binned about having my poorly thigh looked after. I has binned doing sit and keeping still and letting Gran put the cream on, HAND eating a treat afterwards like a proper dog. The hole is gettering much smallerer and I has finished all my tablets. I hasn't made nearly so much fuss and bother as you did say I might do. Gran finks I worry about being fiddled with cos you worry about fiddling with me. I hexpect you might get a talking to about that fing when you gets back. I does hope I hasn't dunned getting you into troubles.

Because my leg has gotted almost nearly betterer, I has binned allowed to make exerlent fabumazing friends with Mattie, who is a Bearded Collie. We did lots of playing and I did careful spectatoring of Mattie doing somefing called a Scale Jump. Gran was concerned I might fink having a go at the Scale Jump was a good idea, which might mean my very too long legs and bony bits might have a haccident or I might open up my poorly thigh. I can tell you now that clambering over a six foot scale fing is not somefing I plan to do any time soon. It was hard enough working out how to jump over the thirty centipeder gate fing to get to my sleeping place.

August 22
Dear fuge ginger boyman

I fink Gran is very quite surprised about how much of a sofa I can do taking over. Like, all of it. She finks I are a sprawly ginger oaf so I finks you and I has somefing in common. The Cavaliers like to do lying along the top of it, and I did lying all along the seat bit, and played bop-the-Cavaliers-ears whilst lying hupside down on the sofa.

Gran forted I was so funny, and was so actual pleased by my gentle boykin hattitude, that she choosed to sit on another chair when she was watching telly. Although how she managed to keep up with the telly programme with Mattie pretending to be a lapdog all night, I has no hidea.

August 23
Dear Famberly

Gran says you is coming back from your hollibib tomorrow and I will be going home. I are quite very pleased about this because although I has had the most fabumazing time and dunned learning a lot and a very lot, I is knackered now and need a rest.

Gran says I are hofficially Welcome. Back. Anytime. at her house. She was very quite unsure how it would work out because of Roxy and her special knees, and Baillie with his boinging, but it has all turned out quite actual well in the end. Gran finks I are a luffly gentle boykin. And Umble. Being Umble is the most himportant fing of all because Umble dogs do not hupset Roxy's special knees.

I fink Mum is going to get lots of talking-tos about all the fings I find difficult and all the fings Mum needs to do differently. Please bring two actual cars when you come to collect me so me and Dad can do hescaping before all the talking starts. Wot with Mum's and Gran's jean sharing, they could be yacking on for weeks.

And I wanna go home.

August 24

I'm home. I are lying on the bed wot I did miss almost as much as Mum and Dad, and I are remembering how much I do like being in my own home, with my own famberly, and even my own cats. Maybe not that bit. But home is home and it smells like I do remember it, and the garden is my outside space wot I don't have to share with bonkers Baillie or bossy shrieking Cavaliers. And I can do gettering in the back door without a hescort or the 'Don't Be So Redickerless' words.

Dad and Mum smell of salt and suntan cream, and other strange fings, but I are sure once I has done having a few more strokes and ruffles they will start to smell betterer quite very soon.

All the cats have dunned coming in for their dinners tonight wot Mum is very quite relieved about. Gipsy-the-Cat can do epic sulking when she actual wants to, and sometimes she does bogging off and being Fishally Hoffended. But she has comed in. Mainly cos I fink Vera ranned out of tinned food and had to move onto giving them the dried stuff, wot Gipsy doesn't count as dinner.

It's honly good enuff to be pinched out of the larder on the sneaky-sly.

August 25

Now I are back from my hollibobs and settled back in my quite very own actual house, I has had some time to fink about my hexperience staying with the Dog-Hexpert. I has dunned learning a lot as well as it being actual fabumazing fun. So, here is my Forts on Being a House Guest. I do fink that probababbly staying at Gran's is a bit very different to staying with other peoples, but as I has only stayed with peoples who fink Dogs Is Himportant and a Pri-Orry-Tree, like Jill and John and Gran-the-Dog-Hexpert, I cannot be saying for certain wot is actual normal and wot is very not.

You will have to do making up your own actual mind.

*****FORTS ON BEING A HOUSE GUEST*****

When you is a house guest it is very himportant to work out who is in charge and do lots of being-very-friendly-luffly-boykin to them. With Gran-the-Dog-Hexpert this was quite actual easy cos she do not do living with anyboddedy else, mainly cos they aren't dogs. With the doggies it was very much harderer to work it out. Iona forted she was in charge of the door and Baillie *was* very actual in charge of all the toys, but the honly fing I can say for sure was that it wasn't actual me. I aren't keen on being in charge so that suited me very actual well.

Working out wot order everyfing happens in is himportant. At our house, sometimes Mum will have a cuppatea and then do giving me my breakfast, and sometimes the other way round. At Gran's everyfing happens the same actual way every day at the same time. So it was cuppatea, medicines for the ancient Cavaliers, then wait an actual hour, then breakfast. From a doggy point of view this is fabumazing and all Gran's dogs know when it is Time. For. Breakfast. But if a hooman does phoning Gran up at five to eight o'clock, they can do forgetting about talking to her about plans for the weekend cos all the dogs do start doing a lot of Complaints to the Management about it being breakfast time.

I don't do barkering very actual often. Not doing barkering at Gran's was super-himportant because she has a new neighbour. He knew Gran had lots of dogs before he moved in, but now he do keep complaining about it. He is every somefing beginning with B you can actual say in one sentence. He makes Gran-the-Dog-Hexpert's life a misery, and he leaves *his* poor doggy in a kennel all day when he goes to work. Wot barks. So he is a somefing-beginning-with-B hippycrit as well. And Gran feels very quite sorry for his dog and will be Doing. Somefing. About. It. actual soon if fings don't change.

Any hooman who forgets to shut a door or lock the gates at Gran's will die, and is also never, ever, hever allowed to visit again.

All of Gran's dogs are really, wheely clever. They can all do tricks or hobedience and stuff like that. Even the Cavaliers do Working Trials and scaling six foot fences. It is all very quite himpressive ... and worrying.

The food at Gran-the-Dog-Hexpert's house was fabumazing. She does all the raw diet stuff, and everyfing was homemade and measured and weighed. I used to fink Mum was a bit actual hobsessed about wot I do eat but Gran takes it to a whole new different level. Mum was a bit actual worried I might not do eating, but Gran did her magic you-wil-be-happy-fing and I eated everyfing I was gived every single day. Gran finks I has binned being gived a little bit too much food at home cos she did weighing it all out. That might be actual why I don't always eat my breakfast at home.

I are trying very quite hard to forget wot a tricycle is. Gran takes some of her dogs for a walk or a trot with a tricycle. And wot is actual worse, is that they seems to henjoy it! I are sure I would actual need ferapy if anyboddedy in my house suggested this was a good hidea. I didn't know they hexsisted before, and if anyboddedy tells Mum about them, I will be sulking for-actual-ever.

I aren't being lied on. No matter how much the Cavaliers fink this is a good idea. They all pile on top of each other and forted I might like to join in. I did decline their kind offer. Cavaliers pile up. Lurchers spread out. Which is a good fing cos I gotted the first five feet of the sofa and they all choosed to sleep on the last twelve inches wot was lefted.

Kennels and Runs are actual very more okay than I did fink they might be. I wasn't in there that often but it was warm and very quite comfy with lots and lots of blankets. And although I couldn't actual get out, none of the other dogs could get in. And try and do lying on me.

Being a house guest means you has a chance to do checking out wot facilertys other people have. Gran has long, lush, bouncy grass at the bottom of her garden, and I did love having a stretch and a roll about in this. I has had words with Dad about this because we don't have any grass in our garden a-very-tall. He isn't keen. He says I will digger it up and I don't know how to use a lawn mower. He is very missing the point. I don't want it mowed, and a few holes would make it more hinteresting. Dad says I need to persuade Mum, then - and that there is 'fatchance' of that happening.

August 26

There's somefing stuck in the chimberly and Mum is all in a flap and a bother about it. Dad finks it's the wind making the whistling sounds Mum can hear, but she is Not. Convinced. Every so often, she suddenly yells "there!" or "can't you hear it?" and leaps up and runs around pointlessly as if that will help or make Dad hear it. It has binned my himportant work to run around hexcitedly with her. Dad can't hear nuffink with me and Mum prancing about; partly cos his hearing is hawful but mainly now cos he's stuck his headphones on to avoid listerning to Mum's sudden 'that noise' yells, and demands that he Do. Something.

Mum says that, tomorrow, when everyboddedy has goned to work and the house is quieter, she is going to hinvestigate the chimberly and find out if she's going mad. Dad says he already knows the answer to THAT question right now, and she do not need to spread soot all over the house to find out.

I aren't sure if that was the hexact wrong fing to say or a very actual quite fabumazing idea of Dad's, but when Mum satted down and gived Dad I'm-gonna-hide-your-ketchup looks, everyfing wented terribibbly quiet.

And then we all hearded it. Even me. I tried to stick my actual nose up the chimberly but everyboddedy fort this was a bad idea, especially when I did a fuge sneeze and splattered sticky, sooty, snot all over the wallpaper. I was not popoola after that, and me and Gandhi and Frank, who also did decide that somefing hinteresting was happening up the chimberly, gotted hejected from the office.

Mum's founded a lamp and put it in the fireplace to show the birdy how to get out, and now she's trying to do sitting quietly and patiently (which she's actual rubbish at), so everyboddedy has had to leave the actual office for the rest of the evening until the birdy comes out. Dead or alive, Dad says. And could it hurry up cos he'd really like to check his hemails.

Dad is quite very actual lucky he's not banned from the whole actual house, Mum says. Dad says he's being realistic. Mum says he's a cruel, horrid-somefing-beginning-with-B. It's been like watching a game of ping-pong cos they isn't speaking to each other, and I are supposed to be passing messages between them wot is himpossible. Cos I are a dog and I don't speak Ingerlish and by the time they has said "Worzel, please tell your father" or "Worzel, please hinform your mother" they has already dunned hearing it and coulda saved me the trouble of being rudely hinterrupted from my snooze by all this Worzel name-saying. I aren't a go-between. I are a Lurcher who is now going to exit stage left and go and lie on the bed away from the bickerickering.

August 28

When we woked up this morning it was quite very hobvious that the birdy had dunned getting out of the chimberly. And from the queue of cats with their noses hunder the door and their bottoms in the air, it was hobviously still alive. After we did removing the would-be murderers from the hallway, Mum opened the door.

So the good news is that when the chimberly sweep comes next month, he won't have nearly as much work to do as usual. The bad news is that, well, the same fing, really. As well as the bird escaping from the chimberly, so has a quite actual lot of soot. And the birdy has dunned spreading it around the place. It also looks like it tried to have a paddle in Dad's half-drunked cuppatea wot he hadn't finished before Mum threw everyboddedy out of the office. Cos there was tea and soot and all different mixtures of the two everywhere. Mum says the last time she saw this much mess was when the previously ginger one was a toddler and decided to paint the kitchen with Vaseline.

Mum says the bird is a Starling. Although I has seen lots of birds on fields or flying about – and I did once nearly have a too-close-hencounter with a fuge seagull – I has never actual binned this close to one before. And ... who the Heckington Stanley decided that birds should have sharp, pointy sword fings on the front of their faces. This seems like a very actual bad hidea and has halmost, very-nearly-but-not-quite, made me fink twice about chasing after Pigeons or Crows. I are going to assume that only ickle birds have these sword fings because otherwise I are sure I woulda somehow gotted the message that chasing after birds when they has actual lethal weapons on the front of them was a bad hidea.

Perhaps this is somefing you only find out after it is too actual late to do telling anyboddedy about it. Either way, neither me or Mum wanted to get too close to the sword-stabbering Starling cos it was seriously cross from falling down the chimberly, and getting covered in soot and then tea. Fortunately, the Starling didn't want to come too near to me or Mum neither, and just kept slamming against the window until Mum managed to get it open and then run away in case the birdy tooked a side swipe at her with its sword fing.

August 30
We did spend most of yesterday clearing up the birdy's paintings and footprints and wing-splatters. And the bird poo wot dribbled down one of Dad's Uff-the-Confuser screens. Mum says she was tempted to leave it on there after all the "Please hinform your mother" stuff, but she's decided that as she's planning on sending Dad onto the roof with a thingamejigwotsit to cover over the chimberly pot this weekend, she'd better start speaking to him again. Cos he hates ladders and she's going to have to do a very quite lot of talking and smiling sweetly and threats of no dinner to him to get him Onto. The. Roof.

August 31
I went visiting this week. I has binned to see my Granny Mary and other senior members of my famberley.

In very general, senior peoples like me very much, and I do like them as well. Senior peoples generally sit in one place and do eating cake. They also does not bother about diets or healthy food, and do fink giving me a bit of carrot cake is very actual okay. Mum and Gran didn't say anyfing, mainly because it is very quite hard to give advices to peoples who knew you when you were six without them reminding you about Significant and Hembarrassing Hevents from your Childhood.

I has to say that I did honly take carrot cake wot was offered to me. How-very-ever, Maisie, Granny Mary's dog, did make sure I gotted offered more than I mighted have done because she took a great slurpy lick of the frosting on the top of the cake, and then none of the hoomans fancied it much after that.

I did exerlent being fuge and easy to see so I did not get stooded on, and when I got a bit tired of looking at peoples' feets, I wented into the garden to say hello to Granny Mary's whistling boy. I waited for ages to see if he would whistle but he didn't, he just stooded there. Mainly cos he's actual made of stone which did take me a bit of time to work out. Mum was quite very actual relieved I didn't do peeing up the whistling boy because peoples wot honly giggle at him have binned frowed out of the house and Who. Knows. What. Would. Have. Happened. if I'd done that ...

SEPTEMBER

September 1

The previously ginger one is starting at College today in Norwich. We is all hoping it is going to go betterer than wot happened at school last year, wot was pointless and hinvolved a hawful lot of peoples not doing listening to Mum. This time, Mum says, she has got all kinds of bits of paper on her actual very side if she needs to do having a hargument, so we is all feeling very quite hopeful and positive.

I had forgotted how long it takes someboddedy who is nearly eighteen to get ready in the morning. I fink she would do betterer starting the night before cos she gotted up so blinking early to do her hair and be painting her face so she doesn't look like the previously ginger one any-actual-more, but she did finally make it out of the door and we all didded breathing a sigh of relief.

"Right," said Mum.

As Dad had already goned to work, I did my famberly duty and went and hid. Dad says this is wot you has to do when *any* woman – but very quite hespecially actual Mum – says 'Right.'

'Right' means Mum is on a mission. Wot may or may not be a good fing but it's best to do hiding until you has founded out wot 'Right' it is or fings could go quite very actual wrong.

Today's 'Right' was mainly a lot of flapping around like a headless chicken, tidying up the fuge ginger boyman's room, wot is mostly used as a dumping ground since he went back to Universally and gotted his own house, and hoccasionally as a garden by Mouse when peoples forget to shut the door, and she is having one of her days of forgettering where she is.

But mainly this 'Right' was about finding somefing to do so Mum didn't do too much worrying and having hystericals about the previously ginger one's first day at College. So we dunned all the washing and a bit of gardening, and sorted out some clothes for the charity shop, and pointlessly opened the front door and stooded gazing at the garden, and cooked several fings for the freezer. And then wormed the cats.

Worming the cats is not a spectator sport if you has any sense, cos although it is quite very edercational and hentertaining watching whilst it is going on, once they has binned released by Mum the cats become like hunpredictababble fireworks wot could hexplode in any direction.

That got us to half-past-nine. And Mum was still worrying and trying too actual hard not to look at her phone for text messages about wanting to come home from the previously ginger one.

Heventually, I did take pity on Mum and do reminding and biffering her that the bestest way to stop worrying was to go outside for some fresh air and a bit of a stomp in some puddles, and most himportantly, Take Me For a Walk. Wot everyboddedy does know is the honly cure for pointless worrying and headless-chicken-doing.

I was so actual pleased with my clever and cunning plan, and then so puffed out from my pigeon-scaring exercises, that I did forget the cats had binned wormed.

I would like it to be actual known that I is not a ferapy dog. And Pets as Ferapee does not actual extend to the cats wot need to release their anger about the worming fing. I aren't a punchbag or a pincushion or any of those actual fings. I are a walking-the-dog/change-of-scenery-dog. And I'd be very acual glad if Gipsy could do remembering that fing next time I come in through the kitchen. Right?

September 2

When Mum was in the fuge ginger boyman's room yesterday, she did see Charlotte-the-Spider. Charlotte has lived in the gap behind the curtain rail in the fuge ginger boyman's bedroom for about ten years now. To be actual quite honest, it's probababbly not the same spider but the daughter of the daughter of the daughter of Charlotte, but it's very quite hard to tell spiders apart, I do fink, hespecially if they is related and always live in the same place.

Even if we can't tell the difference between Charlotte and her daughters, there is one fing that sets Charlotte apart from all the other spiders in the house. She is fuge. Ignormous. Look at it this way: you can do making eye contact with Charlotte, which is quite actual unusual for a house spider, even in *this* house where everyfing is a bit weird, and weird is to be actual hexpected and very lived with.

Charlotte is fame-mouse round here for making Hoccasional and Dramatic Happearances. Usually at about half-past-ten at night when Mum is really, wheely hoping everyboddedy will remember that they has homes to go to before there is no food lefted in our fridge.

About half a second after Charlotte pokes her head out from behind the curtain rail, there is always lots of not-manly screams, followed by a fuge collection of words beginning with B, a thundering of teenage feets on the stairs, and a lot of deciding that it's time to go home.

Charlotte isn't wot you'd call a famberly pet: she doesn't cause Mum any problems and doesn't cost Dad a blinking fortune and she's very actual quite helpful, so she's in very general nuffink like a pet. Hexcept today Mum is wondering, now she's tidied up the fuge ginger boyman's room and removed all the dead socks and half-eaten bits of toast and mouldy tea mugs, whether Charlotte is going to be able to find enuff to eat. And whether she should leave somefing disgustering in there to make sure Charlotte doesn't starve to actual death if she can't find any flies. Wot usually live off the dead socks and stuff.

Mum's decided she's not going to do telling Dad about the mouldy cup she accidentally forgotted to remember to collect from the fuge ginger boyman's room. Cos otherwise he will tell her she is redickerless, and Mum will have to admit she has one dog, five cats. And a spider.

September 3

The other actual day, I did have a himportant visitor called Tracie. She does be the person who did very first rescue me. I did stay with Tracie for a little bit before I did come here. Tracie does have four little children. Two of them were very quite exerlent and stooded still and letted me do sniffing them. Then they did hignoring me and gotted on with eating their biscuits and drinking their pink stuff. They has doned so much being with Sighthounds and other dogs that they did fink I was a bit well, quite very actual hordinary. They did say all the plite fings you should say about me being a luffly boykin, but the telly and the biscuits were actual more hinteresting. As far as I are concerned, they can come again!

The other two, though, were freaky, scary ickle peoplekins wot did not do anyfing I could be predictering!

Mum says this is because they are one and two years old, and all babies are into everyfing and do not be knowing very well how to be still. They also don't know that grabbing dogs or tipping over on a Worzel could be frightening or hurting. I are very pleased to say that Tracie did do keeping the ickle peoplekins hunder actual control, and so none of those scary fings did happen. When the ickle peoplekins wanted to have a hexplore, I did shut all the hoomans and the scary toddlemonsters in the sitting room so I could do careful hobserving them through the bars. It was like going to a zoo but the wrong way round.

Then one of them felled in my water bowl and gotted quite very loud and cross, so I did run away bravely and hidded under the duvet with Dad, who did have comforting words about his hopinion of babies. Turns out he was hiding under the duvet from them as well. Mum did fink he was still asleep but he was quite actual not.

It was all very quite special for mum and for Tracie because they do both luffs me very much. Tracie did keep saying "I cannot believe how big he is." I do find this very quite strange because she had not seed me for over a year. Surely, it would have been much more confuddling if I had stayed the same actual size? I is hoping the toddlemonsters grow as quickerly as she finks I actual has, and that they will be starting their hobedience classes soon. There must be good training classes where Tracie do live because the two biggerer children were very most exerlent!

September 7

Mum do say it is not very actual funny when someboddedy you has knowed since they was twelve suddenly manages to be growed up enuff to be having a baby. And be a compertent and capababble parent, and all the fings that you do need to be. Mum says that it was honly last week that our neighbour, Hannah, was playing kick-post on the field behind our house, and Jack, her partner, was painting pictures of Superman, and how the heckington Stanley can they be parents? Cos if they is parents that makes Mum old.

After last week's close hencounter with babies, I has decided that I can wait until their baby, Charlie, is a bit actual bigger before I meets him.

Mum says that's very actual wise, and as he only lives a couple of doors away, she is sure that we can say hello when he is a bit olderer. Like ten, or somefing. Which, at the speed Mum is getting old, will be next week.

I aren't sure if Mum has started doing running up and down the stairs because she's trying to keep up with time wot is flying by at a halarming rate, or whether she is trying to actual convince herself she isn't old and can still run up stairs wot will prove she's still young, but I fink it is fabumazing. I are trying to be a helpful boykin and joining in with the running up and down the stairs, wot I can do in two big boundings.

At first, Mum was very quite pleased that I did careful remembering about Mum going first, and that was clever and himpressive on the way up. But I are not allowed to do hencouraging her with my nose on the way down the stairs. Cos otherwise, Mum will do going faster than the speed of time and possibly reach the end of time by falling down the stairs. She's comed to the conclusion that it's probababbly safest to haccept being old rather than end up being dead.

And we're honly going to do walking down the stairs from now on.

September 8

It's the previously ginger one's 18th birfday today and she has becomed a Hadult. Being a Hadult means you is fishally growed up and expected to look after your own fings and do your own washering. I fink the previously ginger one might be the honly proper Hadult in this house; Mum can't find her driving license or her passport, and Dad do not even know how the washering machine works.

Apart from saying 'Happy Birfday,' I has got to do a Hannouncement and a Confession. I has been trying to work out wot to do about this, and now seems like a quite very good time. The previously ginger one isn't actual quite previously ginger any more. All that black stuff in her hair is goned; she's binned a proper natural ginger one now for about six months, and Mum is very quite actual happy bout that. So am I, mainly because she's stopped sticking those weird hair 'tension-fings-on-her-head-wot-look-like-black-dog tails.' It's hard to be completely actual the bestest of very best friends with someone who looks like they've borrowed hessential bits of doggy hanatomy to make their hair look longerer. Even if they do give me all the crusts off their toast. And put extra bits of butter on them.

For now, I is going to keep calling the previously ginger one by that name in my stories because otherwise you might fink we've gotted another small hooman here.

Dad's having a bit of a panic now; Mum's been being all filler-sofical over the past couple of days wondering where all the time has goned and wot she's going to do with the rest of her life. He says he do not care wot Mum does with the rest of her life but they is NOT doing THAT.

September 9

I found some blue sweets. Found I some blue sweets!

I blue some found sweets.

I sweetsomebluefounds. Sweetswhizzchargebang-highasatoddleroncola-foundsomeblueeeeeeeeeeeswwwwwwwweeeeeets.

The previously ginger one is quite very actual in the Doghouse.

September 10
I did a blue poo. The previously ginger one is still in the actual Doghouse.

September 11
We've had some hupsetting news but noboddedy is very actual surprised. Iris, the mostest hadventourous and bravest one of Stray's kittens, has been hitted by a car. You might do remembering that Iris was the kitten wot hescpaed when she was four weeks old, and decided that she and Worzel were going to be friends, heven though I is fuge and she was ickle, and had more confidence than is actual good for her. When she wented to live with her forever famberly, she tooked Ivy with her, who, apart from looking hexactly like her, is all the fings Iris are not. Ivy is shy and quiet and cautious, and she did promising to lend Iris all her nine lives cos she only needed one, and Iris probababbly was going to need more.

She needs them *all* now, all the hextra ones she can get. All her insides are bruised and squashed, and her vet cannot be saying if she is going to pull through. Which is a plite and not scary way of saying she might do dying. Hoomans do not like to talk about dying so they say fings like 'not make it' or 'touch and go' to mean might do dying. Perhaps they do fink that if they say the words they will make it come true, which is a bit bonkers cos they'd spend the whole time saying "I'd like a squillion miles of garden and forty Lurchers" if that was the case.

Iris' famberly is very actual worried, and her Mum says she hasn't had any sleep for days now because she has binned told to keep watching Iris for signs of her 'going downhill,' wot is a-very-blinking-nother one of those strange 'might-do-dying' fings.

I are very quite pleased to say that Iris' Mum has not dunned saying words and hoping they will come true, or finking that not saying words will stop them happening, and did wot everyboddedy knows makes wishes and dreams come true. She's worked very actual quite hard at hobserving Iris and staying up all night , but mostly following the vet's hinstructions, cos when Iris started to feel more poorly-sick and needed to go back to the vet, her Mum did get into the car very quite quick and do saving her life.

And now Iris has gotted to have her food specially made small and easy to eat, and she's got to do lots of lying around on her Mum and Dad's bed, and even more being carefully hobserved. Which is all more quite actual hard work when you is a hooman and not had any sleep for days. But Iris' Mum and Dad aren't relying on wishes or 'hoping for the best,' and are going to make quite actual sure that Iris gets betterer. But not all the way 'back to her old self,' though, cos it was her old self wot gotted her into troubles in the first place ...

September 12

Frank's getting really, wheely fat, and, until recently, noboddedy has binned able to work out why. At first, Mum did fink that he was catching big fat takeaways from the fields, but to be quite actual honest, Frank is so fuge, I don't fink he could run that far or that fast. Then we did fink that p'raps he was going in through other people's cat-flaps and eatering all the neighbours' food, but Mum has checked and is sure that isn't happening. And he isn't beating up any of the cats here for their food cos we woulda heard the screaming hystericals and general squababbling and hissing and end-of-the-world noises coming from the kitchen.

It turns out Frank is being far, far more evil and cheeky than any of those fings.

In my house, all the cats get fedded twice a day. Mum puts their food out and then leaves the kitchen and brings me my dinner, and also keeps half-an-eye on me and my dinner because sometimes it's a bit complercated being a raw diet, and she wants to make sure I do eat it nicely and not do burying it in the sofa. All the cats have a certain and special place where they is each fed, and they all eat quietly and then neatly slip off out the cat-flap. Apart from Mouse. Who sits confuddled on the work surface wondering how she got there and trying to remember wot she just did. Then, if Mum or Dad or whoever last had to deal with Mouse's I-aren't-going-outside-when-there's-a-perfickly good towel/bed/ pile-of-washing-just-there disaster remembers, she's gets plonked outside the back door in the vague hope she'll remember wot outside is for ...

Then Mum picks up all the empty cat bowls and puts them in the dishwasher. Nuffink could be simpler or more horganised. Or fail to explain why Frank is getting to be the size of a small caravan. So this morning, Mum did decide to stay in the kitchen whilst Dad did watching me to see if Frank has worked out how to hoperate a can opener. Or somefing. And wot she says she did see was hunbelievababble. Even more howt-rayjus than him opening cans, happarently.

First of all, Frank gobbles down his own actual dinner really, flipping quick. Then he do go over to visit Gandhi and give him a kiss. And a lick. And a general pat and a tap until Gandhi starts to wiggle and squiggle and do the whole down-a-bit, left-a-bit, just there, aaaah luffly ooh! ooh! ooh! and aaahs of an itch that's been scratched. With all the kisses and stuff, he forgets about wot's in his bowl. Then Frank slides sneakily between Gandhi and his bowl, whilst still giving him a bit of a groom and a cuddle ... until Gandhi starts to give him a lick back. Then, whilst Gandhi is busy returning Frank's kisses and licks, Frank settles down to finish off Gandhi's dinner! And because Gandhi is a super-dooper-hunting-baby-bunny-basher, he just bogs off and gets a takeaway, so he's not missing out on food. Frank is eating almost double wot he should, and Gandhi is surviving quite happily on takeaways.

Mum didn't know whether to be shocked or himpressed. Or whether it was a one-actual-off. But it isn't. Frank did it again tonight and now he is in big trouble cos Mum is Onto. His. Game. and it is very actual over. From now on, Frank's getting fed in the laundry room On. His. Own. and then hejected outside until everyboddedy else has finished eatering.

September 13

At least that was the plan. Frank got stuck in the laundry cupboard today, and I has never heard any noise quite like the one he did make to let everyboddedy know he wasn't happy about this actual fact. He let out a yowl that was hearded over the telly, the washering machine, and the previously ginger one and Mum harguing about wot was a reasonababble time to be picked up from a party. It was so loud that everyboddedy did stop wot they was doing and come running to see who had gotted their leg chopped off. Apart from me. I did running away bravely in the other direction. Loud, hunexpected noises are not my area of hexpertise. Pretendering to look for toys on the landing is my specialist subject when loud and hunexpected and frightening noises happen. Turns out Frank quite very likes the warm whooshy air of the tumble dryer but isn't so keen on the washering machine's spin cycle.

After he had binned rescued and clucked at by Mum, and was sittering recovering from the shock of all the kerfuffle and hystericals, I did come downstairs and chase him out of the cat-flap. For scaring me half to actual death and being not-as-big-and-brave as I fort he was. Mum says I was mean, and some other stuff about kicking-a-man-when-he-is-down. Well, Frank isn't a man, he's a cat, and he hobviously needed some fresh air and time to consider whether makering screaming yowls is an okay fing to do when you is General Frank of the Ginger Militia.

September 14

At teatime today, Frank was sittering on the table. As I walked past, he very deliberately and with NO CLAWS tapped me with his paw. If he'd dunned mean and beastly attackering my hiballs I fink I might have hunderstood. Now I'm just a little bit confuddled and very, very worried ...

I aren't chasing Frank ever, hever again. He keeps lookering at me like he's plotting somefing. And then turning his back and hignoring me. It's all very quite uncomfy in the nerves and panicking area of my boddedy.

September 17

Iris is out of the woods. Apparently. I did not know she had been tooked to the woods, which I don't fink is the bestest place to be keeping a poorly-sick cat. I are suspecting this is one of those Don't. Mention. Dying. fings again, and I are hoping it means she's gonna get betterer. In my mind being out of the woods is a bad fing, and means it's time to go back on your lead and do being good and going home and all the fun is very actual over. And there's likely to be some practicering of heelwork and someboddedy saying sit. Being out of the woods is quite actual NOT a good fing for dogs, but it is for cats who has binned not well a-very-tall, and means she is going to be okay.

continued page 121

Gandhi the bunny-basher, all growed up.

Me and Lola do very hagree that playing in fuge puddles, is fabumazing. Even if we do make the car soggy.

Booful Lola.

I did rip a hole in my leg wot nearly putted the kibosh on my famberly's hollibob, but the Dog-Hexpert saved the day.

Visiting Harbour Cafe is always fabumazing cos I get sandwiches and sausages.

Looking for water in the watermeadow before Merlin wented and looked on the other side of the road and got tolded off by Pip.

Booful Worzel.

My finking and fortful pose. I don't seem to be able to fink with all my feets on the ground.

Out on the beestrip practicing hobedience where noboddedy can see me.

I could win prizes for my lying-hupside-down skills, Mum says.

Racing kite through the puddles once the farmer did finally clear a bit of his sugar beet

My noo neighbours are very fusey-tastic about playing. Especially kite. kes and Maisie fink about playing a lot and a lot but their boddedies don't join in.

This is my friend, Maisie ...

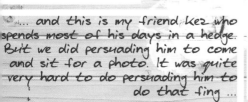

.... and this is my friend kez who spends most of his days in a hedge. But we did persuading him to come and sit for a photo. It was quite very hard to do persuading him to do that fing ...

... and this is Kite who is very actual fusey-tastic about everyfing.

My new favouritist puddle since the farmer buried my old favouritist one.

ris-n-Ivy are still very actual nearly
dentical, hexcept Iris had a hargument
with a car.

I are very quite exerlent at playing
with toys. When I want to. And
when noboddedy is lookering or
expecting me to do bringing it
back all the time. There is billions
of toys lost all over Suffolk
because of actual me.

I can quite very actual fly!

Hexploring in Corny Wall.

Don't tell Grandad about me sleeping on the bed. I don't fink I was supposed to do this ...

September 20

Over the past week or so, I has been being a very good boy. So good that Mum was beginning to quite actual worry. On my walks I has been exerlent at recall and fabumazing at checking-back. I hasn't doned any bogging off, neither. I hasn't eated anyfing I shouldn't have, and even Mabel is coping with me being in the kitchen. Mum, being Mum, did decide that maybe there was somefing quite actual wrong with me, and was starting to wonder if I should have a visit to see Sally-the-Vet ...

Last night, though, there was a hatmosfear here. Mum was due to have a hoperation on her wonky foot today, wot everyboddedy kepted telling her was very nuffink to worry about. But Mum was actual doing a lot and a lot of quiet worrying about it. Dad didn't notice Mum worrying and do proper asking wot's-up? questions, so then as well as the worrying, there was also a bit-cross-about-Dad-being-an-hinsensitive-husband hatmosfear as well. I decided to do keepering out of the way, and did lots of watching peoples with my eyebrows.

This morning Dad still hadn't got the hang of sensitive or fortful or caring when we gotted a phone call cancelling the hoperation cos of an hemergency. Mum decided to treat today as a trial run and gived Dad some tips about How To Do Better Next Time. He says he didn't notice Mum was feeling wobbly and that he isn't a mind-reader. I find this very hard to hunderstand. *I* noticed. I are fabumazing at noticing when fings is not quite right. Dad needs to learn that if I is lying in my own bed and doing careful hobserving then there is probababbly somefing actual up. Wot he should be noticing. And saying somefing about. I'll do the noticing and he can do the saying somefing about it cos I are as very rubbish at saying somefing as he is at noticing.

Hanyway, since the hatmosfear has goned, I has felt MUCH actual more like my own very self and today I has dugged a fuge hole in the garden, knocked over the runner beans canes, and chewed some reading glasses. Normal service has been re-zoomed. I was hoping that Mum would be a bit more actual very pleased about this than she actual is; at least she's not worrying about me being ill any more.

September 21

It's a blinking good job Mum didn't have her hoperation yesterday cos I don't fink we coulda coped with all the dramas we hadded here last night if Mum hadda been hopping around on one foot and off-er-ead on painkillers. And she definitely wouldn't have binned able to call the fuge men in green with their flashing lights when Dad forted he was having a Art Attack. A real one, not a that-was-a-bit-of-a-shock one. Well, Mum had a bit-of-a-shock one cos she fort Dad was having a real one, which did surprise everyboddedy cos Dad doesn't do being ill.

Dad's got one ear that doesn't work and one knee that stops him doing dancing, and that – as far as he is actual concerned – is about as broked as he is prepared to be. He doesn't get headaches or tummyaches, just the very quite hoccassional and demanding bout of

Man Flu, but since Mum discovered Day Nurse, he isn't allowed to have Man Flu any more. Dad doesn't take painkillers or vitamins. He says he has a horange and a banana every day and that's good a-very-nuff.

So when he wented a sort of grey colour tonight and had a really, wheely bad pain in his chest, he saided absolutely nuffink. But you know that hatmosfear fing? It turned up again, and cos Mum is not Dad she noticed. And then she really panicked when Dad didn't do hobjectoring, or saying Mum was making a fuss and to stop being redickerless, when she said she was calling a hambulance.

Last year, when we had the green men with flashing lights in our house for the previously ginger one, it was my himportant work to stay with Dad. So I tried to do the same fing this time but I got tolded I must be shutted away. Being shut away when there is a hendless stream of green men with flashing lights knocking on your door is quite actual hard. So every time a new lot arrived I did taking my chances and sneaked up to be with Dad. At one point there was five green men with flashing lights, and their bags wot are fuge, and some electric-beeping equipment, and Mum and me, and Dad (hobviously) in the bedroom. I did quite very well at keepering a low profile, but then another green flashing man tried to come into the bedroom and we ranned out of floor space, so I had to sit on Dad's head cos that was the honly space available. Then I got stucked in the kitchen with the cats. None of us was very actual himpressed.

After they all bogged off to the Opital the previously ginger one rescued me from the kitchen. And the kitchen from the hapocalips that was about to be me – and Mabel. Then, we wented back to bed and waited and waited and waited ...

Heventually, Mum phoned and said that they'd given Dad six different painkillers and none of them had worked, but most himportantly, Mum could have him back, cos the doctors all gotted very bored and not very hinterested in him once they maded sure he wasn't having a Art Attack. Mum was ever so very NOT pleased. She says Dad was still in pain but now unable to walk, cos giving him all the painkillers he NEVER takes was like putting Dad on the outside of seventeen glasses of cider, and he can only really drink three before he gets silly, anyway. And all this at four o'clock in the morning was just wot she needed.

And now, Dad's passed out on the sofa, Mum's pacing up and down in case the painkillers decide to making him sick – and we still don't know wot's wrong with him.

September 22

Yesterday morning, Mum had hystericals at Dad's Gee-Pee, wot is a doctor that knows everyfing, not just about Art Attacks. And Gee Pees don't get bored when you have somefing else actual wrong with you. When Dad pitched up at the doctors, he had a sore-poorly chest and the worstest hangover in the world from all the painkillers, but between Mum, the doctor and Dad doing groaning at the right times, they know wot's wrong now ... and it isn't good news.

Dad did have Near Death by Carbonara. Or Strangulating Spaghetti syndrome. Or a load of other very not good pasta-based jokes that the fuge ginger boyman keeps texting to Dad and making him laugh, and then yowl cos it hurts. Basically, Dad camed in late from work, and at half-past-nine shoved his dinner down himself so blinking fast, and eated so much that his hinsides wented into a fuge spasmy cramp. And apparently it IS fugely painful and very quite like a Art Attack. But also quite very hembarrassing. And noboddedy is allowed to make any more jokes about the way to a man's Art Attack be through his wife's dinner, fanking oo kindly.

September 23

Happy Quite Very Actual Birfday to my Granny Mary, who is 92 today. Dad says I will be in the serious Doghouse for saying how many numbers she's got after her name, and I aren't supposed to do telling you that fing.

   Oops.

September 24

Dear Farmer-wot-owns-the-field-near-my-house.

I has spended all summer making sure the pigeons and seagulls do not do eatering your sugar beet so I do fink it is honly fair that you do diggering it out of the ground now so it can go and make cakes. And so I can have my puddles back.

   Sugar beet is very exerlent if you want to be doing himpressions of Rhubarb and Custard with your ears flappering about, and very quite hexciting for teaching sleepy partridges to fly, but it isn't a puddle. And at the quite very actual moment, I would like a fuge ignormous puddle to make up for all this blinking rain.

   Puddles is the honly really useful fing about rain, wot I don't like happening to me, or on me. So, please can you do actual hurrying up with your tractor machine? Please?

Fanking oo kindly

From your luffly boykin

Worzel Wooface

September 26

One very bad fing about Mum's hoperation being delayed is that Mum isn't going to be able to do Panty-Mine this time round. They is just about to start doing rehearsals and Mum doesn't know when she will have her hoperation, and after she's had it dunned she won't be able to do dancing for about a month.

   Normal people wot is hexperienced at doing actoring and Panty-Mines might be able to do catching up with learning the dances, but not Mum. Mum has special knees when it comes to dancing, and it takes her forever and ever and extra lessons and loads of being very yelled at to learn the dances. She doesn't fink she will be able to cope with the stress of it all, and she do not be wanting to hinflict her special knees and her poorly-toe on the people wot is actual In Charge this year. It's hard enuff trying to horganise everyfing without worrying if one of your actoring people will ever be able to walk again. So Mum is going to do Front of House this year, which is when you tell peoples they must do buying raffle tickets and have a play on all the games, and bossy stuff like that. Dad finks it sounds like a perfick job for Mum, and does that mean he can have his shed back, and not have to do lighting or help Mum learn her lines, or do hendless cooking and wonder if Mum is going to ever come home again? I fink Mum might be a little bit actual disappointed about not being in the Panty-Mine but it's very hard to show this when your husband is dancing round the kitchen cheering.

September 28

Dear Man who has comed to do gardening for Mum

I are sorry you does not like dogs. Your two friends do fink I are a super chappy and I has dunned having luffly strokes after we did the exerlent hignoring fing. I know you does not want them to know you are scared of me. They might fink you are being silly or not manly and I does hunderstand you do not want your friends to know this. You has dunned a exerlent job of pretendering in front of them. But you has not fooled Worzel Wooface.

I can tell you doesn't like me. Your shoulders keep trying to disappear into your ears and your voice has gonned a teeny-ickle bit higher that it usually is. And you keep waiting by the gate and having a quick looky round to see if I are actual about before you come back in.

Hunfortunately, I cannot work out why you doesn't like me. Is you scared of me or does you want to do hurting me: I aren't actual clever enuff to do decidering. Or trusting. Some hoomans hurted and frightened me when I was a ickle puppy and since then, whenever I has metted hoomans who does not like me, I really, wheely need them to do going away big-time-badly.

That is why I keep barking at you. Cos I fink you are going to hurt me, or yell at me. So, if it is actual quite okay with you, I are going to do staying in the house today. Hunder the table behind a stairgate so neither of us do gettering any more scared or shouty.

I aren't mean. Or nasty. I are just very actual quite terrified of you. Sorry about that fing.

Your luffly boykin

Worzel Wooface

September 29

****RULES ABOUT COMING TO MY HOUSE****

- 🗐 New peoples are scary.
- 🗐 Everyboddedy is a new person until I decide that they is not. Even if I has metted you six times before.
- 🗐 In very general, I only want to meet one new person at a time.
- 🗐 If you is a small hooman, you still has to do following these rules. I aren't a learning hexperience; that's wot toys are for.
- 🗐 New peoples should do standing still with their hands in their pockets, and do exerlent hignoring me and pretending to talk to Mum.

📜 Mum isn't doing this talking bit because she's sick of everyboddedy wanting to say hello to me and hignoring her. Honest.

📜 The longer you hignore me, the quicker I will decide you aren't new.

📜 If you feel me hencouraging you with my nose, that is your cue to get the yummy bit of cheese wot you did bring for me out of your pocket.

📜 If you did forget the cheese, I are quite happy to go back to number one whilst you go to your car and get the piece of cheese so we can start again.

📜 If there is no cheese in your car, this isn't going to work. Come back tomorrow. With cheese.

September 30

Mum cooked carbonara for tea tonight. I are pleased to report Dad didn't do having a Art Attack. And noboddedy else said anyfing stupid, wot might have gotted the saucepan frowed at them. I forted you'd probababbly want to know.

OCTOBER

october 1

This week I has binned Dad's dog and not cos I did rolling in poo or other actual fings wot Mum says is disgustering and very Dad's department, but because Mum has been away looking after the Dog-Hexpert's doggies.

Being Dad's dog is great mainly when it doesn't hinvolve cow poo and then baths. I get to go to work in the Harbour Office and do Management, and then go to the beach.

Dad says it's been a hinteresting hexperience seeing how much *not* like a terribibble two-year-old I has becomed and I are like a quite very actual different dog. I don't do nearly so many Complaints to the Management and I are much more settled. I seem to have growed in confidence, he says. I are quite very pleased he has dunned noticing this and not saying that I has growed in the waist department, cos Jill, who is Lola's Mum, and works in the Hoffice, has a pocketful of posh treats wot I has decided are good enuff for Worzel to do eating.

Today, after we finished our beach run, I was allowed to do walking back to the car without my lead on, which is somefing he did never, ever, hever fink I would be able to do. But I did exerlent padding along beside him and not being distracted, or looking like I was going to go bogging off after the Poodle wot had just arrived at the beach. It was all very satisfying and proud-making he says. And a blinking sight easier on his blood pressure.

october 4

Mum's back! I has founded out why she did bogging off and it is all very quite hexciting. She hadded to go and look after the Dog-Hexpert's doggies cos George – one of the Cavaliers, who is glamorous and hobedient – was being a Film Star. According to Gran he was playing a dog called Alice. Wot is definitely a girl's name. I don't fink anyboddedy should tell George this because in real life George is quite very actual manly for a Cavalier, and I don't fink he would happreciate everyboddedy knowing he was being a girlie. I expect when the film comes out he will do a lot of saying it wasn't him and noboddedy-can-tell-Cavaliers-apart-cos-they-all-look-the-same-honestly-it-was-Isobel. George says being a Film Star is very okay because you get shedloads of treats, though there is a hawful lot of hanging around and doing the same fing seventeen times. I fink I shall stick to being a luffly boykin: at least I get to keep my own name. And not have to cover up my gentleman bits. Or be called Alice.

october 5

We saw a canoe with some peoples in it on our walk today. Mum wented all misty-eyed about this and started finking romantic forts of drifting down a river in a canoe with me. I fink this is a fabumazing idea. Both of us would get very quite wet and one of us would be very quite not happy about this after five minutes. Mum's having second forts now: maybe it isn't so romantic, after all.

october 6
Have you pinched our pepper pot? Can you check? Mum's losted ours and she's driving me flipping bonkers going on and on about it. I has not got the pepper grinder. It isn't in my bed, I hasn't buried it in the garden. Noboddedy has sneaked into the house to pinch it. Everyfing has binned turned hupside down here today lookering for the blinking fing, and we aren't going for a walk until Mum either finds it, or accepts she is going nuts. Or someboddedy is trying to convince her she's going nuts, which is a bit more worrying, cos ever since Mum sawed the film *Gaslight*, she's had nightmares about it.

   Dad has not got the pepper pot. He doesn't like pepper, and probababbly do not know wot it even looks like. The previously ginger one hasn't gotted it. I don't know how she knows this but I do know from all the words beginning with B that if she gets accused of having it in her bedroom One. More. Time. she'll throw the hentire contents of her bedroom down the stairs. Like she did when she was six and I wasn't around, and I are quite very keen she doesn't do it again. The fuge ginger boyman hasn't binned home and 'borrowed' it for his new house cos Mum says she's seed it since he's been gone.

   So that means that either someboddedy is trying to convince Mum she's going nuts and then she'll start panicking like she did last year about the squiggle on the kettle hincident wot she's still not forgotted about, or she's going nuts. So if you has seed the pepper pot, please can you let me know where it is? Cos I wanna go for a walk before I. Go. Nuts.

october 7
I fort the pepper pot fing had binned forgotted when Mum gived up and went and brought a new one. But now she's losted that one as well! Dad says she's driving him bonkers-crazy, and can she *PLEASE* shut up before he loses the plot? Wot Mum losted long before she lost the pepper pot.

october 9
Dad founded the pepper pot. It was cunningly disguised as chocolate sprinkles. We're all very quite carefully not mentioning that there's still one missing, though, and the words 'Pepper' and 'Pot' have now becomed words beginning with 'B.' Bepper Bots are also banned from the conversation unless you want to do living in the shed with Mabel.

october 11
Today, somefing very quite special did happen. Hattie-Hazel Princess-Poo-Pants did come to visit! We did have a fantastic walk and an ignormous

game of bitey-facey on the sofa, and we was so very actual pleased to see each other and gotted quite very over-hexcited and panty-puffed-out.

We did get a exerlent update on how fings are going with Hattie-Hazel. The cats in Hattie-Hazel's famberly mostly do living upstairs nowadays. Apart from when they is sitting on the top of a shed teasing Hattie-Hazel and generally making everyfing a lot noisier and complercated than they need to be. Cats teasing Lurchers is not helpful, and in very general leads to a disaster or needing much higher fences, at least.

Hattie-Hazel's Mum and Dad do report that she is their perfick doggy and has carried on with her chattery-muttering demands, and loves to cuddle. She is still Orrendous at pinching food, and all the hoomans reckon that will never actual change.

One fing that has changed is, well, Hattie! She is about six inches taller than when she did live here, which was a fuge shock for everyboddedy. Mum says her guess at how old Hazel-Hattie was must have binned completely wrong and her finking that she was fully growed was even more actual wrong. She is now nearly as big as me and not a little Whippety girl a-very-tall. Apart from the muttering and the liking to wear pee-jimjams. That bit's still all Whippety but the rest of her be a slinky, super-fast Lurcher.

october 12

Granny Mary, who is Mum's gran, is in the Doghouse. Yesterday, she did do falling over. I do falling over all the time and I don't end up in the Doghouse for this actual fing but then I is not 92. I will probababbly be in the Doghouse for telling you how old she is again, and I has only dunned this fing because it is himportant to remember it, otherwise none of this will make actual sense ...

Hanyway, Granny Mary has this button fing she presses if she does falling over or feeling un-very-well. And then someboddedy phones Mum or Gran-the-Dog-Hexpert to tell them to go and stand Granny Mary the right way up again. And get very shouted at because she does not want the button to tell Mum or Gran she's falled over. She doesn't really want the button a-very-tall to be quite actual honest, but she doesn't have a lot of choices cos if she falls over, she can't get up.

When Granny Mary felled over this time and pressed the button, neither Mum nor Gran was at home to get the call. Granny Mary was very happy about this because it meant the person on the end of the button hadded to phone for the fuge green men with flashing lights. Granny Mary says she would prefer to be stooded up by the fuge green men with flashing lights because she does not want to bother Mum or Gran-the-Dog-Hexpert. Both Mum AND Gran-the-Dog-Hexpert has tried very actual hard to hexplain that the National Health Service is a bit hunder actual pressure cos of the poxy guv'ment, but Gran says she is ninety-two and she's paid her taxes, and then Mum and Gran-the-Dog-Hexpert bang their heads on the tables and walls.

So, once the fuge green men with flashing lights had dunned standing Gran up, she decided she was very quite alright, fank oo very much, and she was going to have a nice rest. More himportantly, she was Not. At. Home. to receive visitors.

Unfortunately, she forgotted to communercate this small detail to Gran-the-Dog-Hexpert, who came back to her house, found the message on her ansaphone, rang Granny Mary in a panic, got no answer, panicked some more, screeched herself round to Gran's in the car and then banged and banged and BANGED on the door. Then she really, wheely panicked when there was no answer, and decided that Granny Mary must still be lying on the floor. Gran decided to do her own actual version of Working Trials scale jumping, even though she is nearly seventy, and climbed over a six foot fence to get to the back garden. You can probababbly himagine that after struggling with this fing. she wasn't that actual pleased to see Granny Mary sitting in her chair watching the telly and eating a chocolate biscuit ...

Being a himportant member of my famberly means I get hinvited and hinvolved in almost everyfing that happens round here. I are very quite actual pleased to say that I was not hinvited round to referee the fuge hargument and hindignant jean-sharing yelling wot happened next. Dad was, but he did plitely decline Mum's offer to come and help, and hidded in the shed. I fink he was worried Mum might find him there so he did also quickly cover most of his actual self in fibreglass as well. My Dad is super-quick-finking clever and wise like that.

Mum says that even though Granny Mary is ninety-two, she is as sharp as she was when she was twenty-two, and she hasn't losted any of her marbles. (This is a good actual job, I fink, cos if she'd lefted any of them lying about, Gran-the-Dog-Hexpert woulda picked em all up and frowed them at her, especially when Granny Mary tolded off Gran for whining about climbing over a six foot fence, as "the paramedics managed it.")

I has dunned quite a bit of worrying about wot will happen the next time Granny Mary falls over, but it turns out that, once everyboddedy did stop yelling about being unfinking and stoopid, and Gran-the-Dog-Hexpert not breaking her neck climbing over the fence, and "you're not in a Jane Austin novel and you can't flipping well decide to be not at home to visitors," they did all come up with a cunning solution.

Next time Granny Mary falls over, *Dad* will be in charge of putting her the right way up again. Wot serves him right for leaving Mum to sort out everyfing again. Maybe Dad's not so wise and clever after-very-all ...

october 14

It's hofficial. Mouse has got behaviour problems. Sally-the-Vet said so. Now, I don't want to cast nasturtiums on Sally-the-Vet: she was asked the question "wot is wrong with this cat?" and she answered it. But the fing is, I don't fink it is actual necessary to have four Hay Levels and seven years at veterinary college to be able to work out wot's wrong with Mouse. I are a dog and I coulda dunned it. I dunned it months ago, to be quite actual honest.

At the moment Mouse has a hidentitee crisis. She either finks she is a Monkey or part of Mum's boddedy. She clings to Mum and won't let her do anyfing or be anywhere if Mouse isn't attached to her clothes in some way. This is all very well when Mum wants to do chillering out or having a cuddle, but getting dressed with a cat trying to balance on your head is himpossible. It's all getting a bit time-consuming. And cost-re-fobic.

Before Mouse was pretending to be a Monkey-cling-on, she was doing all kinds of very strange fings. Like playing hide-and-seek with herself and getting shut in a drawer for thirty-six hours. And not hobjectering. Everyboddedy was hunting around for her like mad, and a lot of fings was said about her being missing again and never coming home, and not being able to go through another five years of her being AWOL, and no, we WON'T be going sailing this weekend if we can't find Mouse. And No Dad can't go on his own, and could he stop being a hateful beast and start being a supportive husband? But mainly could he find the blinking cat before Mum goes mad!

Heventually, the hoomans started looking in redickerless places, like wot you do if you're desperate and have runned out of ideas: inside the fridge and under the carpet, and finally one of them opened a tiny drawer, inside a wardrobe, having already looked into the wardrobe six flipping times already ... and there she was, curled up, half-asleep and wondering why everyone was grabbing at her and waking her up when there was nothing wrong with her a-very-tall. And could they all go away now and shut the wardrobe door on their way out?

Mouse has gone through stages of refusering to walk down the stairs, so when it's dinner time, someboddedy has to go and actual collect her or she just yells and whines. Or stays asleep on a bed for two days until someone has to pick her up and put her in front of a food bowl. And then plonk her outside so she can do a wee. Which she does once she's out there but she has this look on her face that says 'oooh, that was a good idea – why didn't I fink of that?' She's crazy-barmy.

And she has sharp claws. Which is where the visit to Sally-the-Vet and the diagnosis-wot-Worzel-coulda-gived came in. Mum can cope with her little bits of weirdness and the scared-of-the-stairs and the forgettering to eat stuff because it's not that far off the odd fings that the other cats here sometimes do. But when you're having a bubble bath and minding your own-actual-business and reading your new Kindle and working-very-hard-at-remembering-not-to-drop-it-in-the-water, and suddenly, out of nowhere, a small grey cat decides to jump in with you, realises she doesn't much like water after all, then hangs on to your belly for dear life like Kate Winslett on the bit of wood in the Titanic film, *then* you go along to Sally-the-Vet.

October 16

Lola is here and she are staying for a week this time. She will mainly be staying here with Worzel and not going to work with Dad, which means she can have a hollibob from her himportant Management in the Hoffice work. I do not fink Lola is really very quite made for Management. She is far too pleased to see everyboddedy, and mostly finks that everyfing peoples say is exerlent. She even finks the most stoopid ideas peoples have, like going out for a wee in the pouring rain, is a good idea.

Lola is quite actual rubbish at being a leader but is very actual good at doing sucking-up. She do do sit without being asked. When Lola does sit, it's like that boy at the back of assembly, who sticks his hand in the air and goes ooooh ooooh oooh and nearly falls over trying to be noticed. And just like the boy in assembly wot mostly gets hignored, so does Lola cos she's really only doing it so that someboddedy gives her a treat.

When her sit-like-you're-going-to-faint-if-you-don't-get-noticed doesn't work, Lola tries 'paw,' and in the most redickerless places. Like when the hoomans are sitting on that special seat in the bathroom. Every doggy, hexcept Lola, does know there is no treats in the bathroom, so I don't know why she do bother.

Lola isn't actual bossy at all. She never tells anyboddedy wot to do, though she do seem to get her own way an hawful lot of the very time. Like last night when she did persuade Dad that he wanted a squiggly Lola sitting on his lap, even if it meant he couldn't see the telly and spended most of the evening spitting out spare bits of Lola that she didn't actual need no more.

On second forts I are going to have to have another fink about this Management malarky, cos Lola seems to have everyboddedy horganised without being bossy or a leader at all. Lola is quite very persistent and fusey-tastic and hirritatingly helpful so peoples just do wot she wants without even realising it. Dad says she's Just. Like. Mum.

october 17
I has letted myself down very big-time-badly. I was out for a walk and was about to be letted off my lead when I did find myself doing sit Without. Being. Asked. I was tolded I was a luffly special boykin and wonderful. But I do not fink I is wonderful a-very-tall. I are shamed of myself, and Lola – who does sit whenever she finks she can get a stroke or a treat out of it – is a Bad Hinfluence. I was so confuddled by this turn of hevents, I didn't even notice the partridges running along the bee-strip until they was about twenty feet away and then they all tooked off at once. And instead of being a hinteresting fing to chase, they did make me jump out of my very actual skin, so I did hiding behind Mum. Who was delighted and finks I are finally coming back round to being her fortful and responsive boykin. I aren't: I was too actual worrying about where that flipping 'sit' came from. And how I can do stoppering myself doing that redickerless fing in the future.

october 18
Over the past few months or so, Mum has binned finking about whether

I would like another dog to come and live with us all the time. When Hazel-Hattie was actual here being fostered, Mum was very, very, VERY quite actual certain it was not somefing she did ever fink was going to be a good idea. Not that Hazel-Hattie was unkind or nasty, it was just that Hazel-Hattie food-pinching was Blinking. Hard. Work. Then me becoming a Hindependent Worzel who don't need no Mum, but needing fuge amounts of work and convincing that coming back and jumping in people's ponds, and then gettering my gentleman bits trimmed, and all the trauma ferapies Mum did need about that fing, made Mum and Dad fink they needed another dog in their life like a hole in the head!

But now that fings are slowly actual gettering back to normal, Mum has binned finking those forts again. Dad finks Mum is hinsane, and has pointed out that one ignormous Lurcher on the boat is redickerless; two would be himpossible. If Mum is finking that, then we need a biggerer boat, HAND to win the lottery.

He do have a point. I need lots of actual space and attention on the boat, and although my actual leaning and balancing skills are fabumazing, I aren't sure how good I would be at doing these if I had comp-knee. And if we felled over, I do wonder how eight Lurcher legs would manage to do untangling themselves before we had to stand up and do leaning in the hopposite direction. It's hard enuff with four legs, I can quite very actual tell you.

Mum did a lot of yeah-butting with Dad, but it turns out that Mum has stopped finking about wot she wants, or wot Dad wants because those fings are easily worked out if it's a pri-orry-tree, and she has dunned lots of finking about Wot Is Right for Worzel.

I love Lola and all my other doggy friends, and it is my favouritist fing in the world having visitors. But this week, whilst Lola has binned staying for a bit actual longer than usual, Mum has noticed some fings that have maded up her mind.

Lola is a perfick house guest. But I get very quite over-hexcited having a doggy visitor. After about three days I do start to do naughty fings, like chasing the cats down the stairs a bit actual more, or telling them off for pinching my dinner. And the number of shoes I has tried to eat has definitely gonned up this week. Mum finks it's cos I are still really a quite anxious boykin: I can do behaving perfickly for a short time, but after a while it all gets quite actual too much for me. And I need my own quiet space and quiet time to do calming down and just actual coping with life. And five cats. Coping with five cats wot are all mostly weird or mad is more than enough for anyboddedy. And I do fink that mostly the cats don't want to be chased down the stairs or feel that coming in through the cat-flap is Mission Himpossible with a giant dose of skidding Worzel on top.

So a decision has binned made. I are going to have visitors and lots of doggy friends outside my home but I are not going to have a brother or a sister. Mum is going to stop secretly lookering at Lurcher rescue websites with pangs and wonderings, Dad is going to not be gettering a bigger boat, and I are going to be a honly boykin. So long as there are lots of playdates and visitors, then I fink this will suit me quite very actual well.

october 19

Very, very quite hoccasionally, Mum and Dad do have a hargument. To be quite actual honest, they is rubbish at it. Years and years of living with the fuge ginger boyman and having to join forces against the World Champion of Harguing Until they're blue in the face mean that they aren't very actual good at being on opposite sides.

Usually I don't do paying much attention to harguments, and disappear to go and find a shoe to chew, but yesterday I did realise that actual sometimes it is worth paying attention, and that there could be betterer fings to do than bogging off and leaving them to it.

First of all, you do need to pick a side. Who is going to win the argument is quite actual not the point. You does want to pick the person most likely to say fings like 'I'm-going-down-the-pub-until-you-stop-wittering-on.' When you hear these words, go and sit by this person and look fortful until they say 'HAND I'm taking-the-dog-with-me.' Then you'll get a walk, HAND a packet of porky scratchings as a quite actual bonus.

If the weather is very rubbish, you will not hear words about going down the pub. Cos they is not stoopid or that cross, so they might say hinstead 'I'm going to the shed.' And then you want to choose the person who is going to be staying in the house cos it's freezing in the shed. And Mabel lives there.

If you find yourself on a fabumazing walk down the pub, it is very quite hessential that you remember you has Himportant Work to do other than eating porky scratchings and saying hello-luffly-boykin to the soppy Rottweiler wot do live there.

The bestest and easiest fing to do is to get a mystery limp. Not enuff of one to start peoples finking about Sally-the-Vet or anyfing too actual drastic like that, but enuff of one so that the idea of walking home is very Not. On. Then the person in the pub will have to do calling the person sulking at home and explain that Worzel Wooface has hurted his foot somehow, and can they both have a lift home, please? And sorry about forgettering to bring home toilet paper. And then harguing about it whilst you was stucked on the loo.

Then everyboddedy will be too busy flapping about the weird limp, and wondering if you do need your poorly-paw bathed, and trying to convince Worzel Wooface that he really does need it *at least* looked at, and running up and down the stairs trying to do this fing, to ever remember that they was having a hargument.

october 20

I has binned modelling for the Harbour Cafe in Southwold so that peoples do know that dogs can actual go in that place and be very quite welcome. They did make me feel super-special and I gotted bits of sandwich gived to me so that I kepted still. And looked like a gorgeous luffly boykin. I do recommend the sandwiches, by the way ...

october 21

All the famberly except for me are off on a weekend hollibob today. At first, I was a bit actual unhappy that I was not allowed to go, but then I did find out two fings wot has dunned changing my quite very actual mind.

First-of-very-all, they is going to one of those places with cabins in a wood. Although this sounds like a perfick place for Worzel Wooface, in autumn-time in our part of the world a wood is a very quite dangerous place for doggies. Not cos it's got killer squiggles or anyfing dramatic like that, but because of somefing called Seasonal Canine Illness. It's a bit of a mystery wot it actual is or how doggies do getter it but it's Orrendous, and so Worzel Wooface is not allowed to go playing in woods during the autumn, wot I are quite actual glad about.

Second-of-actual-all, instead of going to the Cabin-in-a-Forest and being hexpected to learn how to play badminton, I are going to Lola's house. We did do lots of practising in the summer about staying away from home, and I are really, wheely hexcited. I has dunned promising to be the good boykin about staying away from home and it's going to be fabumazing. And I can do playing bitey-facey and zooming around like a loon, rather than doing trying to hit shuttlecocks wot I are certain I would be very quite actual rubbish at.

october 25

Yesterday, Mum did finally have her hexploding toe hoperation. To make her hop, I do fink. She has a bandage on her foot wot does smell very actual strange. I does not like it; it smells of dry very-clean-fings and it isn't a nice smell for a doggy a-very-tall. According to Mum, she is under Strict Hinstructions to do nuffink for ten days. Which means that Dad is hunder even stricter hinstructions to do everyfing. I don't fink this is going to turn out very quite well.

To be actual fair to Dad, he is quite atual good at being Superman when he gets enuff warning. In writing. And he's known about the hoperation for weeks. Mainly cos Mum's been wailing about it. And worrying. And realising her will isn't up-to-date. Dad has been much betterer at noticing Mum's worrying and being helpful and supportive, and for-goodness-sake-you're-not-having-open-heart-surgery-you-stupid-woman. He's fabumazing at stuff like that.

Dad says that the way to deal with hoperations and Mum being hunder Strict Hinstructions, is to do something called Forward Planning, wot is very quite complicated actual finking. He's boughted hindustrial quantities of sausagebeansnchips wot he's planning on cooking every night for dinner so noboddedy does starving to death. and yesterday he tooked me for A Walk. Because he can't do proper hinteresting walking me every day, cos of his work, he decided I was going to have all my walks for this week in one actual go. I is completely knackered now. I can't move. I has been walked into next month which was happerently the Hole Idea. But Mum's had to hop up and down the stairs three times already this morning to get me to go out for a wee, and to have my breakfast, and then to check I was doing breathing. And stuff like that. I fink I will be be quite actual okay though I aren't getting out of bed for the rest of the day. And Mum hopping up and down the stairs is definitely not following Strict Hinstructions.

october 27
Mum says she cannot do facing another night of sausagebeansnchips. So after Dad went to work this morning, Mum did more of the not-following-Strict-Hinstructions and sneaked out to play in the car. Then she started the car and turned the car around and had a little drive, then SLAMMED on the brakes wot scared all the neighbours and made the cats come roaring in through the cat-flap in hystericals. She says she wanted to make sure she could do braking in a Hemergency if she decides she's going to be betterer and ignore the Strict Hinstructions.

All fings considered I fink it would be a good idea if Mum decides she's had enuff of doing nuffink. She's flipping dangerous when she doesn't have actual much to do, and she might decide to try and teach me to do a new trick or somefing. We has a long list of failed new tricks already so I don't really want to do adding another one to the pile, fanking oo kindly.

october 28
Mum says I has to tell you her car is somefing called a naughty-matic. Cos she do not want anyboddedy to fink she is reckless or stoopid, and most himportantly she do not want to get tolded off by a policeman. And then not be allowed to do driving her car any more.

To be actual quite honest, I do not fink this would be such a terribibble fing. Going in the car makes me wobbly and I do shaking. Mum says I aren't allowed to not like going in the car so we has to keep practising doing it until I *do* like it. And remembering to drive to nice places like the beach if we has to go to not-so-nice-places like, well, anywhere actual else, to be very quite honest.

But if I has got to go in the car, I do fink that some rules are very quite reasonababble.

*****RULES ABOUT GOING IN THE CAR****

📑 If you is going in the car, in very general I don't want to come.

📑 Unless we wented somewhere fabumazing the last time. **THEN** I do want to come and we'd better be going to the same fabumazing place again.

📑 Please don't use the hooter, the windscreen wipers or the brakes when I is in the car. They is scary.

📑 On second forts you can use the brakes ...

📖   I does not want to wear my seatbelt cos I can't see out of the window when I does. But I want to go in the back in a crate even less, so I will put up with the seatbelt fing, though I don't like it, and I will sit up really, wheely tall so you can't reach the clicky fing it plugs into. Even when it is raining and your bum is getting wet.

📖   You can't leave me in the car on my own. Ever. Even if you has just gotted out to post a letter ten feet away. I will do jumping up and down and set off the car alarm. And then do refusing to get in it again for a week cos the noise frightened me.

📖   You is not allowed to sing in the car. You may fink noboddedy can hear you. I can. And it's not adding to my overall motoring hexperience.

📖   Humpback bridges are not fun. And they don't make me want to go Wheeee! They do ... but not in the way you mean.

📖   I does not want you to make the car go any faster than I can run. Be grateful I is not a Corgi cos I fink I would still feel the same way about this fing.

📖   I does not want anyfing you is eating. There is a small mountain of very hignored dead chicken nuggets and dried-out chips on the floor back here. You fink someboddedy woulda noticed. And stopped offering them to me by now ...

october 29

Flowers would have binned betterer, Dad says. Or putting up with learning a new trick. But coming out in simperfy with Mum by degloving a dew claw and needing a bandage and being watched, and most himportantly Not. Even. Finking. about doing licking, is very quite actual bad timing. And being hexpected to be lifted onto the bed by Mum so that I can lie next to her and do having a matching limp is not helpful a-very-tall.

october 31

Today is Halloween. It is the day when small monsters knock on our door and ask about Trigger Trees. I do not know where Trigger Trees grow but we has not got one in our garden, and I does not want to be meeting monsters. And it do not matter how many times you say 'it's-just-Alex-from-across-the-road-you-numpty,' I will not do believing you. Alex-from-across-the-road is a small boy with ginger hair wot smells of pizza and his Mum's Labrador. He is not a flappy ghost fing with hairy hands and green hair. Wot is having hystericals cos he's overdosed on red skittles.

So until this redickerless scary stuff is over, I will be mainly hiding at the top of the stairs.

THE TOP OF THE STAIRS

The top of the stairs is the safest place
To hide from people I might not know
To wait for them to show their face
And decide if I want to say hello

The top of the stairs is the bestest place
For Worzel Wooface to watch and wait
For letters to land, or cats to chase
Or pouncing on friends on a play-date

The top of the stairs is the quietest spot
To chew on a brush or commit some crime
Then slip downstairs and pretend it was not
Me, cos I've been with Dad all the time.

The top of the stairs is perfick for me
For hiding, for finking, for eating Dad's shoe
If you cannot find me, look up and you'll see
Worzel Wooface looking at you

NOVEMBER

November 1

Dad's a plonker. Even Dad finks he's a plonker wot is very quite hunusual and not somefing I has ever heard him hadmit before. But peoples who get new hair clippers and don't read the hinstructions, and – more himportantly – don't wait for Mum to read the hinstructions, and then scalp themselves so much that they look like a hescaped convict, is definitely a plonker.

And also in urgent need of a hat.

November 3

Dear Frank and Gandhi

It does not very matter how many actual times you does try to sneak up on my carefully-saved-bitta-nobbly-bone. I will woof at you. I will woof at you all night, even if that means Mum finks there's somiboddedy trying to get into the house.

Could you please be giving up on trying to pinch it cos I really need to go outside and do a wee ...

Love from your luffly boykin

Worzel Wooface

November 4

Our usual postman is very actual quite sensible and cheerful and is hexperienced with dogs. He strolls in, sneaks me a biscuit, curses about the plant pot Mum has hartistically positioned right in the middle of the path wot Dad says is going to kill somebodeddy one day, mostly avoids tripping over it, and off he goes. You knows where you are with a postman like that. You is in your garden, definitely not diggering up the cabbages, just generally having a moment pondering your breakfast and checking out who has visited the garden in the night. It is all very relaxed and predictababble and after I has said hello-Mr-Postman-Mum-says-she-doesn't-want-any-more-bills, we all just carry on with our day.

But every Friday, our usual postman has a day off and then the Other. One. comes.

Mum says there is nothing to very actual worry about with the Other One. But there is. Instead of just barging in and remembering about the stupid plant pot in the middle of the path, the Other One waits to see if I are about.

I do not like people who do pausing. Or checkering. Or concerned hesitatering. Peoples wot do concerned hesitatering scare me. I do find myself doing concerned-but-without-the-hesitatering-barkering-and-rushing-uppering. I must be very actual exerlent at concerned-but-without-the-hesitatering-barkering-and-rushing-uppering because in very general that makes the Other One stay right out of the garden and actual yell for Mum. And look a bit pale.

Yesterday, the Other One broughted a fuge parcel, and because he was too busy trying to juggle the parcel and his machine fing and not trip over the stupid-blinking-plant-pot-you-is-going-to-have-to-move-it-before-you-kill-someone, he did not do noticing me in the garden. So, in he came, and because he didn't do that Orrendous hesitatering stuff wot makes me go all wobbly and himpressive and scared, we did just say hello-luffly-boykin. Just like that.

Sometimes you do just need a bit of luck and a fuge parcel to solve the problem. Dad says this is a major improvement; now when the postman falls over the redickerless plant pot, at least I'll say hello nicely whilst we wait for the fuge green men with flashing lights ...

November 5

Tonight it's Fireforks Night, when hoomans stand around in the cold and dark watching their money hexplode. But fireforks are dangerous and very, very quite actual hupsetting to hanimals, including those wot do live in the fields and the woods wot you don't hear hoomans talking about. I don't fink the fick fesants and foxes are any more actual himpressed with fireforks than I are.

I do fink that fireforks should honly be setted off on Fireforks Night and honly by peoples wot know wot they are doing. Like at big, horganised displays, or somefing. Apparently, it's traditional at this time of year and all about celebrating someone trying to do blowing up a big house. I has to say that if someboddedy tried to blow up our house, Mum and Dad probababbly wouldn't do having a party and eating marshmallows, so it is all a bit confuddling and a bit quite actual bonkers-crazy if you fink about it.

The cats are not at all very keen on Fireforks Night.

For an actual start, Fireforks Night is the one night when Mum hinsists that all the cats do come inside, and the cat-flap do be shut. And a fuge box is putted in front of it so Frank can't use his hignormous boddedy to stage a cat-prison break-out by smashering through the cat-flap. In my hexperience, cats seem to have the same actual idea of how to be dealing with hunexpected noises. Run. And Hide. When the first bang went off, and Frank biffed himself on the box blocking the cat-flap trying to get out, and had a fortful moment wondering where his brains had goned, all the cats decided that hiding in the house was going to be the way forward.

Cats is not very himaginative. They all came up with the cunning plan of hiding under Mum's bed at the same time. Well, not at the same time. Very definitely not at the same time. I do realise that this might be quite hard to himagine cos a cat takes up about a foot of space, so there should be room for about forty cats hunder Mum's bed, but it's not true. Ask Gipsy-the-Cat. She decided that hunder the bed was her place and noboddedy else was allowed to share, which is a bit quite actual selfish, though it did mean they was all worrying a lot and a lot about each other, rather than the bangs.

Unfortunately for Worzel Wooface, I did also briefly decide that hiding under Mum's bed might be a good idea. But once you've tried to hide under the same bed as a spitting, hissing terrified ninja furball, who has already foughted off four hysterical hinterlopers and is beyond reason and is also called Gipsy-the-Cat, it is quite actual easy to get your fears in order, decide that any bangs or whizzes are very nuffink compared to the hapocalips going on upstairs, and leave the cats to have their meltdown in private.

Mum and Dad fink their Dealing with Fireforks training (the radio on loud and hignoring my concerned and wobbly face) has binned a fuge success, and that my exerlent behaviour is all down to them.

I fink they might feel a bit actual differently later on tonight: their bedroom looks like, well, a load of fireforks has gonned off in it ...

****STUFF YOU SHOULD KNOW ABOUT CATS****

- The cats is in charge. Even Mouse is more in charge than I are. Cos they've got claws and they say so.
- I are never coming to say hello to the Gipsy when she is on your lap. She can do purring and plotting my death at the actual same time. *You* can only see the top of her head. I can see her face and predict the future.
- Gandhi is not a cat. He is my friend and I boughted him up so he finks he is a dog. He is a terribibble hexample of how fings could be with the other cats. Cos he is not a cat.
- All dogs fink cat poo is food. Sorry about that fing.
- If you don't eat the dead mouses Frank keeps bringing you as a actual present, I will have to do that fing cos otherwise he feels hunappreciated.
- I don't hunderstand why it is okay for you to shout at Mouse for scratching the arm of the sofa, but I are not allowed to.
- The hoption to transport me and a cat in a car at the same time does not exist. We tried it and I nearly, almost, might have, coulda died. Don't make me do it again.
- I do not want to be in the same house as the cats after you has dunned giving them tablets. They take it out on me. Wot is not funny. And you is too busy putting on plasters and repairing your own fingers to notice.
- The dishwasher isn't leaking ... Mabel is.
- We do not be needing any more cats, even though the previously ginger one says we do cos having five is wrong and we need six. Cos six is an even number, and she's weird about odd numbers. Mum says the previously ginger one has gotted enuff letters after her name without adding **OCD** ...

November 6

Today, the fuge ginger boyman is twenty-one. Which probababbly means he isn't a boy anymore. But he's still fuge. And still ginger. And we is very quite proud of the fabumazing man he has becomed.

Mum says if your baby is overdue and you is worried that the Opital is threatening to make your baby come out, whether or not you like it, go to a firefork display. It's about the honly fing they is useful for. If you has tried the spicy food and you has tried the bumpy car rides, and all the other strange fings wot are supposed to get idle babies wot can't be bothered to be borned to come out, wot you need is a fuge rocket going off ten feet from where you is standing. It worked for Mum.

November 7
Dad says that if Mum do not stop nicking his coat to go for a walk, and then stuffing his pockets full of smelly treats he is going to get quite actual cross and selfish about sharing. Today, at work, he putted his hand in his pocket to lend someboddedy a drill bit and ended up handing them an ickle dead fish.

November 9
Yesterday, I gotted to have playtime with Mattie, who is the Dog-Hexpert's Bearded Collie. Mattie is a Very. Good. Girl. wot passed her tracking hexam a couple of weeks ago, so she is clever as well as booful. And very actual hairy. Too hairy. It's quite himposible to play bitey-facey with that much fur flying about, and very quite tricky to tell which end is the bitey-facey end and which end is actual not, especially when you is travelling at supersonic Sighthound speed.

I did discover that haccidental bitey-bum can cause all sorts of actual problems. First-of-very-all, you end up with a load of fluff in your mouth wot won't be spitted out. Second-of-very-all, you get a very actual hoffended Beardie, wot wants to hide behind her Mum. Which caused all sorts of hunexpected problems cos although Mattie planned on hiding behind the Dog-Hexpert, I didn't plan any stopping distance, and so the Dog-Hexpert taughted me all the rude words she does know when I crashed into her.

I wanted to tell the Dog-Hexpert that it was her clever and booful Mattie wot passed her tracking hexam wot caused the disaster, but she was more hinterested in calling me a boney-bum-with-no-brakes. This might be quite very actual true but at least you can do telling the front end of me from the back. And I still can't get the fluff out of my mouth.

November 12
I has just been offered a bit of banana. I do not hunderstand this food a-very-tall. So I has tried to bury it in my bed. It didn't go quite as I did plan, cos although it looked quite firm and meaty, it squished quicker that I did ever himagine. So now I has some squished banana stucked between my toes wot I can't get out, and it's driving me a bit bonkers-crazy. The rest of it is spread all over my bed so I has felt the need to do some rolling in it as actual well. Mum says she shoulda known betterer.

November 14

I are sorry to cast nasturtiums on one of my fellow creatures, but I has decided that fesants are, well, fick.

I know they do manage to look after themselves most of the time, and do staying out all night on their very own (wot I could not do a-very-tall), but maybe they is only clever and cunning at night. Because during the day they is stoopid ... and I has hevidence.

For a quite actual start, snoozing on a footpath wot is used by actual loads of peoples and dogs is a bit very daft. Specially if you do tucking yourself up all cosy hunderneath a nice bit of grass. So noboddedy can see you. Not paying attention to wot's happening above you and allowing a Lurcher to stand on your tail definitely counts as fick, and is very quite actual lacking in the finking-about-the-future department. Like a future where you is alive, for a start. That is just plain being a hidiot.

Fortunately for this fick fesant, the Lurcher wot stooded on his tail was Worzel Wooface. I do not have much of a prey drive. Hanimals that want to be chased by me have to make it really, wheely clear that this is wot they want, generally by having hystericals and squealing, HAND running away. Then I get the message that this is wot is hexpected and will do my bestest running about aimlessly, before I forget wot it was I was chasing in the first place and get distracted by a flutterby or somefing else more hinteresting. But this fesant did not do this. He just looked very quite surprised and a little hoffended before he squawked 'geroff-my-tail-you-oaf.'

Mum tried to show the fesant how to be a bird and had a right flap. About there being somefing-wrong-with-him-and-was-he-sick-and-should-she-try-to-take-him-to-Sally-the-Vet? Turns out the only fing the fesant was suffering from was wot Dad called Near Terminal Stupidity.

Anyway, after I tooked my foot off his tail, the fesant remembered to do wot he should have done about ten seconds previously and heaved himself all burpily into the air, shouting at everyboddedy as he staggered off. If it had been me, I would have putted less effort into the amateur dramatics and I've-just-been-stooded-on-by-a-dog-the-WORLD-was-going-to-END-but-it-didn't-cos-it-was-Worzel-and-he-can't-catch-nuffink-even-if-he's-standing-on-it, and more effort into the flying away bit.

I don't fink whoever hinvented fesants was very fair. The main difference between a bird and every other hanimal is that birds can fly. Mum says it's called a USP, wot stands for Unique Selling Point. I reckon it stands for Up ... Stagger ... Poo ... which is wot the fesant did as he flewed away.

November 15

You might actual fink that Dad is a saint and perfick, and does putting up with Mum as a kind of punishment for somefing he did quite actual wrong in a previous life.

And in most cases you would be actual right.

But Dad is also a hoarder and a disaster, and Mum's gonna kill him if he doesn't chuck away some stuff. Soon. Tonight, they has spended an hour looking for a disk for Uff the Confuser wot Dad promised to put in a safe place. Like he promised to do six weeks before that. Mum heventually founded it down the back of the office desk in amongst the cobwebs and the God Knows Wot, where Frank had shoved it when he tried to clear some space to put his fuge and ignormous self. In front of Uff the Confuser is where Dad keeps everyfing he can't be bothered to put away. Or finks is a 'safe place.' Or wot he is currently using to stop Frank from lying where it is warm and guaranteed to get attention. Attention like 'get-out-of-the-WAY' is better than no attention at all, and a sure way of getting more dinner.

Mum says he is teaching Frank somefing called negative behaviour, but mainly, please, please, PLEASE can he frow away some stuff and stop hoarding, and put the disk somewhere where she can find it? So they don't have to do this again next month!

November 16

It's a very quite actual true fact that one of the cats in this house is either bonkers or super-clever. It is also, Mum says, beyond disgustering.

When Mum camed downstairs this morning, one of the cats had cunningly and very actual skilfully filled up a bowl with wee. I are not kidding you. Noboddedy can work out which cat it was because it could have been any of them. Apart from Gipsy. Gipsy is hexcused being haccused of anyfing redickerless because she isn't. Redickerless, that is. Scary and grumpy, yes. But deciding to wee in a food bowl is very quite actual not her style.

I are actual himpressed. And also quite confuddled. Why would a cat fink this was a good idea?

Mum is having a crazy flapping fit now and going round the house checking every bowl, cup and pot we do own ...

November 18

I has been trying to explain to Lola about socks. Lola finks everyone should be as hintersted in socks as she is. Even if she has showed you the same sock a billion times already. Mum loves Lola, but last night even she couldn't pretend to be interested in the same himportant and special pink sock forever, so she satted on it and hoped Lola would watch the telly instead. It didn't work; Lola just watched Mum sitting on the sock for the rest of the evening instead.

The whole point of socks, I fink, is to annoy Mum. To do this, they work in cunning pairs called Odd and Lost. Lost Sock's job is to go and hide as quickly as possible. If it do decide to hide in the house, it needs to choose somewhere disgustering where Mum doesn't want to look. Under the bed or down the back of the washering machine are very rubbish places to hide because Mum always looks there. Sneaking in amongst other people's private fings wot Mum doesn't want to know about is a quite actual good place to hide because Mum will dread wot she is going to find in the private place even more than she will be pleased to have found Lost Sock. There are places in teenagers' rooms where It's. Better. Not. Knowing.

Ideally, Lost Sock should try to escape from the house by way of a Sock Smuggler. Sock Smugglers come in many different shapes and sizes. Dad-shaped Sock Smugglers take them down to the boat and then kick them off at the end of the day so they fall down into the bilge. Teenage Sock Smugglers take them to parties, drink too much actual beer and then can't remember their name, let alone how many socks they did take with them. Or wot colour they are. Or be able to hidentify their own socks. A really clever Sock Smuggler will not only smuggle our Lost Socks out of the house, but also smuggle someone else's Lost Socks in! I never do deliberate actual sock smuggling but sometimes I do forget myself and do burying them in the garden. Or flinging them all hexuberantly into the napple tree ...

Every year or so, when Mum is bored of shoutering at Odd Socks and the box is completely overflowing, she do decide she's Had. Enough. Of. Them. and do frowing away all Odd Socks. Then all of the Lost Socks come out of hiding because they has wonned the Game of Socks. And everyboddedy puts socks on their Christmas lists so that the game can begin again.

I fink socks are supposed to be fings wot humans put on their feets to keep all their toes in the same place. And to keep them warm. But mainly I do fink they do wear socks to stop Lola collecting them up and delivering them to hoomans when they is trying to watch himportant sport or *Downton Abbey*. Again. And again. And again.

November 21

We has noo neighbours! So I wented to visit them and do introducing my actual self. They is all rescue Labradors. Maisie gotted rescued from a biscuit tin I do fink but her famberly are trying their bestest to do making-sure-there-is-less-of-Maisie.

I was a luffly boykin and did say hello in my bestest wriggle-along-on-my-belly-being-ever-so-very-humble. Maisie did try to do this-is-my-garden stuff, and tried to tell me to Keep Off The Grass. Then she had to go indoors until she remembered her manners. After that she was actual very keen to be my bestest friend and cried when I didn't play with her. It was very quite confuddling.

As well as Maisie, there is Kite, who is quite very young, and Kes who is quite very ancient. Kes likes to trot around but not join in with the bitey-facey. He has more himportant fings to do because he can't do reaching all the bits of him that need a urgent scratch or itch; he likes to walk along, half-in and half-out of the hedge, using it like a great big brush. Sometimes, because he is very quite ancient and wobbly on his legs, he ends up more in the hedge than he did mean to be, and more hupside down and stucked than he wanted, and then it is kindest not to look at him trying to find out where his digger-nitty has goned.

Kite, like most young Labradors, do not have any digger-nitty. She do not need it cos she has fuge dollops of fusey-tastic forts. Her Mum does say she is mostly made of plastic in her joints but this do not stop her henjoying life, and the most himportant fing is that she is happy and kept fit. Keeping Kite happy and fit is somefing I could be very quite exerlent at. She has a big back garden wot is all fenced off so we can do tearing around and playing bitey-facey, and try to remember to stay off the flower beds. I are very quite rubbish at remembering to do that at home so I hope Kite is betterer at it than me.

After I had teared up their previously perfick lawn, Mum did decide it was probababbly best we left before they all clapsed in hexaustion. When it was time to leave, Mum did ask Kite's Mum to put all the dogs that weren't me back inside the house. Because Maisie had binned a bit bossy about her garden and did finking about not sharing nicely, Mum says it is himportant that I wasn't stucked on my lead when all the other dogs were loose. Cos otherwise I might feel a bit trapped and worried and we could all do falling out big-time-badly. Hopefully, when we has hadded some more playtimes together, we can all do relaxing about that fing, but the first time it was himportant for my confidence and keeping everyfing safe.

I fink we will be hinvited to play again, but Dad says I should wait until they has all recovered and someone works out how to keep Worzel Wooface and Kite off the flower beds; she is as bad at that fing as I are.

November 22

Mum finks I has learned some hobedience wot she is all proud and chuffed about. And I did get luffly pats and scritches for being an exerlent boykin.

She finks I has learned to walk backwards when she says 'back.' Well, I has. Very quite sort of. When Mum camed in through from the kitchen carrying Gipsy and said "Back," she is quite right that I did take three very worried and actual quite anxious steps back. And when she saided it again, I was only too actual happy to do being hobedient and a luffly boykin and take more actual steps backwards. But I aren't sure I have completely very actual learned 'back.'

Wot I has learned is don't-make-no-sudden-moves and don't-take-your-eyes-off-that-cat-for-a-second-if-you-do-plan-to-still-have-two-hiballs and get-very-carefully-out-of-the-way-of-Gipsy, who as well as trying to dig out the inside bits of Mum with her back feet, was hissing and spitting and doing serious Complaints to the Management.

So Mum is kind of actual right: I has learned to do 'back.' In the same situation, I fink you probababbly would have learned that one actual very too.

November 24

The weather here is horribibble. Cold and windy and getting to be a very lot like winter. I are in complete hagreement with Mum that 'outside' is not a happening fing today. Fortunately, the previously ginger one has dozens of parcels due for delivery today so we have a marvellous excuse to stay in.

OOPS

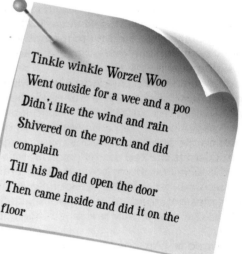

Tinkle winkle Worzel Woo
Went outside for a wee and a poo
Didn't like the wind and rain
Shivered on the porch and did complain
Till his Dad did open the door
Then came inside and did it on the floor

November 25
Dad just sawed a cat outside wot looks exactly like Mouse. He got all hexcited and dragged Mum to the window to have a look.

"Look," he said. "That looks just like Mouse!" "That's because it IS Mouse," Mum said. Now they're harguing cos Dad says it *can't* be Mouse cos she never goes outside.

November 26
This playing with the Noo Neighbours is going really, wheely well, and Maisie wot got rescued from a biscuit barrel, is getting very quite actual a bit fitter. Mum isn't, though, cos now I has decided I like to go round to Maisie's house for playtime and Boot Camp training, Mum is doing a very lot less walking and a hawful lot more standing around drinking coffee and yacking. She reckons that's okay cos it is cold and dark and miserable all the time now ... and the neighbours have got a summerhouse she can hide in when it's raining. And I are not to do telling Dad cos he finks Mum is being heroic and walking Worzel wotever the weather.

November 27
Gipsy-the-Cat is coughing this morning. She's binned breathless for a few days now but it isn't a chest hinfection cos Gipsy's had loads of those and we know wot they look and sound like. Mum's pretty actual convinced that there is somefing wrong with her heart and doesn't know wot to do. Gipsy is eleven now which isn't actual very, very old for a cat, but wot with all the chest hinfections she's always getting it's not hunexpected. But it is a fuge worry and it's making Mum sad.

146

The fing is, Gipsy is our Top Cat. The fings that are himportant to Gipsy are being In Charge, bogging off and hunting. Staying indoors is not one of Gipsy's pri-orry-trees. When our famberly goes on hollibob, Gipsy goes on her own version of a hollibob and bogs off until we all come back. This is Orrendous for the peoples who do looking after our cats cos they want to do checking that they is all very alright every day. And that hinvolves seeing all the cats and counting to five. But Gipsy just doesn't come in when we is away and Mum has to tell people to only panic when they can't count to four.

Gipsy also hates taking tablets. When Mum does worming, Gipsy bogs off for at least two days until she decides to do forgiving Mum and wants some different food to the birds and the baby rabbits she have been catching. And Mum knows (the Dog-Hexpert has two Cavaliers wot have dodgy hearts cos their stoopid breeder didn't do the proper checks on their Mums and Dads before they was allowed to be borned) that the treatment for dodgy hearts is tablets, twice a day, every day, at the same time.

Well, that is never, ever, HEVER going to work with Gipsy-the-Cat. The first time Mum tries it, she's gonna bog off for two days. And the second time she tries it, Gipsy will probababbly bog off forever and ever. So Mum's got a horribibble and difficult choice to make: keep her indoors forever. Or let her do dying.

November 28

Everyboddedy here has dunned lots of talking and finking about Gipsy-the-Cat today, And even though Mum knows there is a treatment that could keep Gipsy's heart going, it will be horribibble for her and ruin somefing called her Quality of Life. Quality of Life is the fing that makes it very actual worth getting up in the morning. Gipsy isn't hooman, she's a cat. She can't go off and be a confuser programmer instead of a hunting-bogging-off cat, and keeping her indoors will be too hawful and pointless.

So, tomorrow, Mum is going to see Sally-the-Vet to find out how we can keep Gipsy-the-Cat comfy and as happy as she can be for the rest of her life, however long that may be. But we won't be trying to stick tablets down her twice a day and keeping her indoors all the time so we can do this fing.

Mum and Dad are really, wheely sad. But they do know they has maded the decision that is right for Gipsy and not for them. It just about makes it a bit easier to deal with when they do finking like that, they say.

November 30

Mum is a hidiot, a plonker, a stoopid know-all. And a little bit of knowledge is a dangerous fing. That's wot Mum reckons. Dad and the Dog-Hexpert says it is hinevitable that Mum would fink Gipsy had somefing wrong with her heart when she's seed hexactly the same fings wrong with the Dog-Hexpert's Cavaliers, and she is to stop doing beating herself up. And calling herself names.

Mum tooked Gipsy-the-Cat to see Sally-the-Vet, and Sally did all careful listening to Mum about heart failure and the Cavaliers, and how Gipsy wouldn't be able to take tablets twice a day, and was there anyfing else that could be dunned to make her life easier and betterer before she died?

And cos Sally is quite very hexperienced and used to dealing with Mum, she did her own careful checking of Gipsy, and said wot Mum was finking about Quality of Life was very quite correct.

But more himportantly, Gipsy hasn't got anyfing wrong with her heart a-very-tall; she's got asthma. Wot can be treated with a quick hinjection every month, and NO tablets. Everyfing isn't perfick: the hinjections are quite powerful and could end up giving Gipsy other illnesses wot will ruin her Quality of Life, but for now, Sally says, there is a treatment and Gipsy can carry on being Top Cat and bogging off and catching fings ... and please can Mum stop crying now?

DECEMBER

December 1

Dear Every Hooman in the Whole Wide World

It's that time of year when peoples do panicking about wot to get each other for Christmas. I don't know if you is finking like this yet but there is one actual fing you shouldn't get anyboddedy for Christmas.

Puppies. Or kittens. Or anyfing with a heartbeat to be actual honest. Puppies and Christmas don't go well together. Peoples fink a cute and fluffy puppy under the Christmas Tree will make everyone feel warm and fuzzy. Well, it might for a day. Then everyone will want to play with their new toys, and Uncle Bob will drink too much cider and trip over the ickle puppy hiding under the wrapping paper, and peoples will leave bits of chocolate and mince pies lying around wot the puppy will eat and then get poorly-sick. And no-one will remember to take the puppy into the garden every forty minutes for weesandpoos cos they'll be distracted watching Doctor Who. Or will have falled asleep cos they eated too much trifle.

If you fink a puppy might fit into your famberly, then I has got a cunning plan. Every day this week, go and stand in the middle of your garden, once an hour, for ten minutes. Even if it's raining or there's something really himportant you want to watch on the telly. If this still feels like somefing you would like to do in January, then wait until then to get a puppy. And go along to a rescue centre because there will be a lot and a lot there. All the ones that peoples fort would be cute and cuddly at Christmas wot they forgotted would still need playing with and training and walking after everyboddedy wented back to work, and that hadn't managed to get housetrained in-between *Doctor Who* on Christmas Day and the Noo Near Party hangover they've woken up with.

Socks make exerlent Christmas presents. Or confuser games. Donations of dog food and blankets to homeless doggies in rescues are bestest of all.

But please don't be getting a puppy or a kitten for Christmas. Fanking oo kindly.

From your luffy boykin

Worzel Wooface

December 3

I don't see Merlin and Pip as much as I used to because they have doned moving, but when I do get together with them it is always very fabumazing. We wented to the water meadow today and I had to do a bit of searching for the water. Merlin decided to do searching for the water under the gate and across the road and into the next field, wot did get him called a few rude names and his name saided over and pver again.

I was hunexpectedly good and managed to not do chasing after him. Mainly because every actual time I begunned to fink about it, Pip decided she was a Sheep-Pip-Dog and tried to round me up. I fink *you* would stay-actual-put as well if she came shrieking up to you whenever you moved.

Heventually we founded the water wot was hidded under the grass, and I did my best lying down and pretending to swim in it. It was all very quite wot I do want from a water meadow: boggy, muddy and splashy! I hope Mum and Louise can get betterer at arranging fings so that me, Pip and Merlin can do seeing each other quite very actual more often!

December 4

Dad's poorly-sick. Lying-around-in-bed-coughing-and-spluttering-and-moaning-poorly-sick. He's caughted the boybug that's going round the harbour. None of the girl-people at the harbour have gotted it, just the men. Mum says none of the women has got it because they haven't got blinking time to get it, seeing as all the men are lying around whining about dying. I has been keeping Dad comp-knee on the bed and making sure that the pillows are horganised, and licking his sweaty bits. Wot there are lots of. Dad says I aren't helping, and could I bog off cos I'm hogging all the duvet, and having a wet tongue stuck in your too-hot armpit is even more hunpleasant than the medicine Mum keeps shoving down his neck.

Dad reckons he isn't going to be poorly-sick tomorrow. My version of mopping his fevered brow is revolting and nuffink like it is in the films. Mum's version of nursing is to yack endlessly at him about fings that need doing round the house when he's betterer. She hasn't had him stuck in one place and unable to escape for ages so he's getting endless Ideas-for-the-Garden every time she brings him a cuppatea.

December 6

****Himportant Sigh-and-Tiffic Discovery****

Soap is not actual food. Even when it is wrapped up all pretty in paper to make it look Worth Hinvestigating. It tooked me ages to get the paper off and chew the sticky tape and spit all the tiny bits of plastic out of my mouth. And then fight my way through the hard plastic decoration box. HAND the cardboard flowery container.

It tastes disgustering and definitely isn't wot I want for Christmas, so Granny Wendy is very quite welcome to it. I've only chewed it a little bit so I don't fink she'll notice ...

December 7

We has had a plumber-man in our house this week. Plumbing is somefing I fink I could be good at. It generally seems to hinvolve a lot of scratching your ears and poking the ground and digging about trying to find the hidden fing-wot-turns-the-water-off. I are exerlent at all those things. Apart from the finding bit. In very general, I am rubbish at Find the Missing Fing, even though it is usually me who has hidded the fing wot has got lost, like one of Mum's wellies which has been goned for over a month now. Dad says it's probabbly buried in one of the billion holes I've digged in the garden like everything else, but to be actual honest I can't remember. Once I've buried somefing, I lose hinterest.

We didn't find the wellie when we was playing hunt the missing stopcock, wot is supposed to be somewhere outside our house but actual isn't. In the end a man with a metal detectoring stick came to hunt for it, and there was more scraping and finding of secateurs wot had been lefted in the hedge. But no stopcock. And no missing wellie.

After a lot of sighing and cuppateas, Mum and the plumber-man decided to give up on turning off the water and instead do dealing with the blocked seat fing in the bathroom, where the humans read magazines and do fortful gazing into space in the mornings. Apparently, there is somefing stucked down it and it's got Beyond. A. Joke. Everyboddedy has binned blaming each other for putting somefing down the chair in the bathroom and blockering it, and even I begunned to get worried that I might have dropped the missing wellie down it. So I decided to have a quite actual proper look for the wellie under the bed. And also hide from the clanging and banging and 'Good-Grief-wot-the-heck-is-THAT!' coming from the bathroom.

It turns out there was nuffink quite a-very-tall down the loo, apart from forty years of 'Get-your-nose-out-of-that-Worzel' wot I wasn't allowed to hinvestigate. And definitely not the wellie. And it turns out we don't have a stopcock neither so a man from the waterboard is going to come and dig a fuge hole outside our house. I dunno why he's bothering, to be quite actual honest; I've dug hundreds already. He could use one of those ... and maybe he'd find Mum's wellie.

December 7

Mum says she not sending Christmas Cards next year and it's All. Gandhi's. Fault. And mine, although I fink I has been very quite hard dunned by. Gandhi was the naughty not-so-ickle hogpig thief. He did steal a bit of my breakfast which was a yummy bit of beef wot I should not have lefted lying around. I should be more like a Sighthound in this department, happarently. I are not like most Sighthounds. I like to fink about my dinner for a bit rather than wolf it down like it's going to hexplode in ten seconds. So I quite often look at it, or get distracted by somefing interesting happening in the garden, or ... Mum says it drives her bonkers-crazy. She wishes I would just eat it. Quite very often she picks it up and puts it away! She finks that I will eventually get the message that I must eat it when it's gived to me or I will have to wait till teatime. She is wrong about that fing. I just forget about it and wait for chicken wings in the evening. Because I are on a raw diet wot needs to be carefully balanced to be healthy, Mum says that I can't eat just chicken wings. I can. I has showed her this lots and lots of actual times. But then my poo goes all white and crumberly and gets complercated to get out of me, and Mum gets worried I are going to get all bunged up, so she leaves the chunky meat down so that I do eat it ... heventually.

That's probababbly a lot more information than you did ever actual need but anyway, that's why Mum lefted my chunky bits of beef in the bowl. And then Gandhi nicked a bit. On a normal day this would be a good actual fing from Mum's point of view cos Gandhi pinching my dinner is a quite very good way of gettering me to get on and eat it. So I came rushing into the room to woof at Gandhi about not pinching my dinner but he runned off with a bit. A great big, oozy lump. Then he leapt onto the office table with it, slid about on all the bits of paper there, and finally crashed into the nice neat pile of Chistmas Cards Mum had done writing. And dropped the bit of beef right on top of them. And then growled at Mum for finking she might want to remove him. And then did shaky deading the beef so that any Christmas Card that wasn't covered in bloody gunk had a good old sprinkling. After Mum had removed Gandhi from the office table with the piece of beef clamped between his teeth, and dumped him on the back step with quite a few choice words about him not being helpful and also a hogpig fat lump.

December 9

I has binned fabumazing again. I wented to a Christmas Fair. It was all Dad's idea. 'He'll love it,' he said. 'It'll be great fun!' he said. I fink he wanted to fall asleep in front of the telly without worrying I was eating his eye-pad, which is four-times-more-blinking-expensive-than-a-Kindle-Worzel-don't-you-even-fink-about-it.

I dunno why he worries about it that much. Falling asleep in front of the telly when you is Home Alone with Worzel Wooface is very actual easy and no trouble a-very-tall. Mum does it ALL THE TIME when Dad's at work ...

Hanyway, we wented to this Chrstmas Fair and it was NOT great very fun. And it weren't luffly. It was bonkers-busy. There was fundreds of other doggies there, which was quite good, though there were not enough time to say hello luffly boykin, and there was two fuge – and I mean FUGE – Mastiffs there wot I wanted to say hello to, but Mum and the man did decide we'd crate a hincident so we had to do serious backing away from each other, which meant we nearly gotted muddled up with a marquee-tent-fing wot didn't fall down. But it tried quite very actual hard to, and there was a lot of clutchering at tent poles and panicking.

All the time I was in the crowds I did careful walking near Mum, and apart from the Mastiff hincident I was exerlent at spotting the gaps and wriggling through them.

But then I gotted my foot stooded on. By a type of person called a Silly Cow. Who then decided to add Hinsult to Hinjury and called me a stupid-somefing-beginning-with-B-dog. Mum *was* gonna smile and say sorry-it's-a-bit-crowded, but when the SIlly Cow called me a rude name, Mum moved her mouth up and down and muttered fings I couldn't hear.

We went to the pub after that. Mum put her coat on the floor and I did my curling up on it wot I has binned taughted is the right fing for a luffly boykin to do, and that maded peoples say 'ahhh' a very lot. Several peoples came up to me and said I was the bestest-looking dog at the whole fair, and didn't I have incredibibble eyebrows?!

My foot is very quite alright, fanking oo kindly for asking, although if it's true wot peoples say about your ears burning when other peoples are talking about you then the Silly Cow's ears must be burnt to a frazzle, and have falled off by now.

I are tired now. All those peoples and dogs did be very actual over-stimulating and hexausting.

December 12

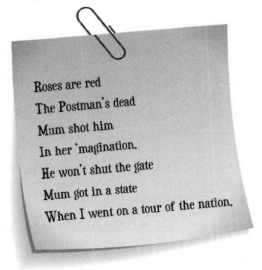

Roses are red
The Postman's dead
Mum shot him
In her 'magination.
He won't shut the gate
Mum got in a state
When I went on a tour of the nation.

Nation is probabbly a hexaggeration. It was really three gardens up the lane, then three gardens down the lane, and a hawful lot of zoomies round and round the green doing exerlent hignoring of Mum calling me.

Then I wented across the road and peed up a few gates and several pot plants, and finally ... heventually ... agreed that gettering out of the man-who-finks-Mum-is-a-bit-nuts' garden might be a reasonababble fing to do.

When I did fabumazing wait-wait-wait-don't-you-dare-even-fink-about-it-wait and wented back on my lead, she said I was a good boy.

I won't do repeating wot the postman was called. It aren't fit for plite comp-knee.

December 13

When Mum sawed the postman this morning she did telling him off about the gate fing. I do feel quite sorry for the poor man. First of all, he has to do not tripping over the redickerless pot in the garden; then he has to remember my biscuit, and today he got a Piece of Mum's Mind. Noboddedy does want a piece of Mum's mind: you only has to see wot it's dunned to her brain to know that bits of Mum's mind are dangerous. And scary.

When the postman had finished being Talked To, he did pointing out that it was his day off yesterday, and it was probababbly one of the relief post peoples wot work when things get quite actual busy at Christmas. And also that he's binned delivering our letters for nearly ten years now, and as he's managed to avoid tripping over the stoopid pot in all that time, he is clever a-very-nuff to remember to do shutting a gate. But he would pass on Mum's Piece of Mind to the peoples back in the Post Office.

I fink Mum and the postman might be friends again heventually. And I know he did shutting the gate, cos I checked.

December 14

Mum and the postman are definitely friends again. Well, Dad hopes they is, cos his wallet got raided this morning so that Mum could leave the postman a Christmas Present in a card, and now Dad's got no money for his dinner.

December 18

I've just discovered somefing very quite actual Hextra-hordinary. Dad has Got A Dad. I know Mum has Got A Mum cos they're always yackering on the phone, and she's also the Dog-Hexpert so I can't get away from the blinking woman. But I did not know that Dads could have Dads.

And I've just founded out that we is going to visit Dad's Dad for Christmas! Apparently, I will love him and he's got my eyebrows. I aren't sure why I should love someboddedy who has pinched my eyebrows ... Dad says he's got the ones I will grow into when I is very quite old and wise, but he says it's probababbly best not being the first fing that is talked about when I do meet him.

He lives somewhere called Corny Wall. It's a long very way away and I has to get used to somefing called Hills. And Cows. Cos he lives near a farm. The cows I aren't too actual worried about. The himportant fing with cows is to pretend that you can't actual see them, and don't ever, HEVER look back. If you look back, they fink this is permission to follow you, and then Mum panics and remembers how big and fick they is, and could they please Please. Go. Away.

Hills I aren't too sure about. The last time there was any mention of hills round here Mum wented to do the sponsored three peaks fingy and her foot hexploded, and she nearly couldn't walk again and wailed a very lot about never-being-the-same-again and I'm-going-die. And stuff like that. So I are a bit actual worried to be very quite honest.

Wot with the hills HAND the eyebrow fing.

December 20

Seeing as I are going to be doing visiting for Christmas, I has dunned some very careful finking about it. Just in case anyboddedy has any funny or stoopid actual ideas about wot a dog might like to happen at Christmas.

****MY TWELVE RULES OF CHRISTMAS****

hohoho I will not be wearing a hat, Or antlers, or a costume of any actual kind. I does not like them at all and if anyone else tries to persuade me to wear one, I will be staying under the table until next year. I does know that some doggies like to wear them but I are not one of those doggies. Unless you has a costume made of fox poo and mud. I is NOT wearing it.

hohoho If you do be planning to dress up any cats in a Christmas jumper I do be wanting to watch ... and bark. There is plenty of plasters in the medicine box. Gipsy-the-Cat says if you go near her with a Christmas jumper you will need stitches.

hohoho All food dropped on the floor is mine. Unless it is sprouts in which case, there is no way I is being your personal hoover and you will have to be dealing with it yourself. I can't promise not to tread on it before I reject it, though, so I suggest you do pick it up quickly before someboddedy slides the hentire length of the kitchen on it. If you does drop mince pie or chocolate on the floor, you do has to be picking these up HIMMEDIATELY, or Mum will have the vapours and hystericals in case I do eat them.

hohoho I do be hexpecting my normal walk and run-around on Christmas Day, even if you has eaten and drunked too much and can't very actual move off the sofa. I will not be wearing a hat for this walk (see rule one) or tinsel. You can do wearing these things if you do very want.

hohoho I reserve the actual very right to stand in front of the telly to watch any dogs wot come on. And if they do barkering, I will do woofing back. If the dogs on the telly do going for a walk, I will be wanting to do this fing, too. Even if it's midnight.

hohoho I aren't watching Queenie unless she do be having the Corgis with her. In which case, I do be referring you to acutal rule five.

hohoho If you do drinking-too-much-cider-falling-over-and-lying-on-the-very-actual-floor, then this is a hinvitation for a game of bitey-facey. You do have chairs and sofas to do your clapsing on. If you do lie on the floor for a long time without moving, it is possible you will get stooded on or I will assume you are a new bed.

hohoho The actual concept of a lie-in is lost on me.

hohoho So is a hangover.

hohoho I is happy to open the Christmas presents but I cannot be doing reading the labels, so if you does not be wanting me to open them all, do not be asking me to open one very actual spercific one. It is all or nuffink.

hohoho Visitors is welcome so long as they do be understanding of the very actual rules above. Especially if they do bring cheese or are clumsy at holding plates wot have sausage rolls on them.

hohoho You might very actual want to stick a note on the chimberley for that person with a sack and a beard and a ho-ho-ho ... he is likely to lose his wellies if he do try to get in that way, and he will be leaving the same way he did come ... probababbly quite very quickerly.

December 23

Corny Wall is NOT a long very way away. It's on a-very-nother blinking planet! It must be cos we were in the car for ever and hever and I are very quite sure we must have falled off the earth and gotted to the moon, the amount of time we was driving.

We was in the car for such a actual long time that I managed to quite very sneakily work out how to get my seatbelt off. Without making no fuss or noise, and without chewing it or hundoing it from the bit where it attaches to the car or nuffink. Mum has got absolutely no flipping hidea how I managed to do this without turning myself inside out, but once we arrived, the harness and the seatbelt were lying on one bit of the back seat. And I was lying on a different bit of it. Dad swears on everyfing that is himportant to him, hincluding his boat, that he had very nuffink to do with it. So it definitely wasn't him. Everyboddedy is just hoping it was a one-off and I won't work out how to do it again.

It is very quite late now so I has not been able to do having much of a look round, just a quick wee in the garden and saying hello luffly boykin to Dad's Dad. Who I are very allowed to call Grandad. Grandad lives with a Nangel called Wendy who is not Dad's Mum but a brave lady wot turned her life hupside down to come and do marrying Grandad a few years ago. As well as being a Nangel, Dad says she must be bonkers-crazy, but she is very quite happy with Grandad, even if Grandad is quite actual set in his ways (according to Dad), and fings like running water haven't made it to the house in Corny Wall yet.

December 24

When the sun camed up this morning, I did get to actual see Corny Wall, not just do smelling it in the dark.

The most himportant I has noticed is that it's all on the wonk and then a bit actual more. Everywhere goes downhill. Even if you do fink you is going sideways you can find yourself going downhill. The honly way to avoid going downhill is to make a really, wheely fuge effort to go uphill. It's all very confuddling and needs a very lot of finking about.

For a luffly fit boykin like Worzel Wooface, going downhill accidentally is not a fuge problem but for Mum with her too big bottom and 'I honly had a foot operation a month ago, of course I'm struggling' toe, going down was a bit of a disaster, and Dad did quite a very lot of dragging Mum up the hill again and a lot of muttering about her needing to do some more exercise in the Noo Near.

I has not seen any cows, and happarently they is all off in some other fields at the moment so there is no chance of us hencountering them. Mum is very quite relieved about this cos as you has probababbly guessed, she isn't keen on cows. She finks they is unpredictababble and they do that following fing and then stop when you turn round to look at them. And then when you calm down and start to fink you is himagining fings, and then turn round again, they has caughted up with you almost like they has binned transported cos there is no flipping way they can have walked that fast and not dunned making any noise. And then Mum freaks out and has to do actual lots of talking-muttering about don't run. Don't. Run. cos then they'll run and ... Mum and cows aren't a good combernation I do fink. Dad says Mum and cows are quite similar in lots of actual ways ... which is why he's got a shed with a door wot locks so she can't sneak up on him and ask him to do decky-rating ...

The house in Corny Wall is very actual old and is mostly not on the wonk. It's propped up at the front by a lot of stones to stop it sliding down the hill. There is a fuge fire wot Grandad is very In Charge of, and wot is his most himportant and hessesntial work I do fink. He is as hobsessed with his fire as Dad is with his boat. This is fabumazing as far as I are concerned cos falling asleep in front of a fire and being very fusey-tastic about Grandad's hard work is somefing I could do for most of the day. Grandad was quite very glad I did like his fire, and he did lots of joining in with my snoozing in the evening.

I do fink I has maded a exerlent good himpression and I are being hincluded in all the snoozing and eating activities, just like at home.

December 25
Wot I should be telling you about is the fabumazing lunch Granny Nangel Wendy cooked, and about Huncle Keith wot is Dad's oldest friend who did come visiting, and all the hats everyboddedy wore wot I was very actual and carefully not asked to join in with. And all that is actual true. But today has also been worrying and Orrendous and flappy-Mum-making, and a lot and a lot of phone calls.

Lola and Sim have goned missing. Someboddedy opened their gate last night, and early this morning they did hescaping and bogging off. And noboddedy has seed them since.

Jill, Lola's Mum, is having a very quite normal and hunderstandable meltdown and John hasn't been seen since the dogs wented missing cos he's out in the woods yelling and yelling and yelling.

Cos Mum is stucked in Corny Wall and can't do going out looking, she is doing all the confuser work with Dog Lost and letting everyboddedy she can fink might be hinterested know that they is missing and loved, and please can everyboddedy keep a look out?

All I can fink about is that it's December and it's cold, and Lola is very quite actual stoopid and not at all very capable of looking after a couple of socks, let alone herself, in the big, wide world without her Mum.

Please come home, Lola and Sim. Please. Please ...

December 26
Lola and Sim didn't come home last night. Mum's starting to fink I might be useful crashing about in the woods near their home, and wondering if we should do going home and helping with the hunt.

Dad says that is very not a good hidea. For a start he's had too much Christmas cheer and Mum is much, much more useful doing all the interweb and confuser work that she is betterer at than anyone else she knows.

Later on

Lola and Sim have binned found! They is very quite smelly and dirty, and Lola is a hogpig so she's starving, but other than that they is very okay. Some other friends of Jill did wot Mum fort I might be useful at doing and tooked their dogs into the woods where one of Mum's confuser contacts had seed Lola and Sim the day before. And after a bit of racing about and yelling and generally belting all over the place, instead of two dogs coming back, four camed back. Which is such a relief. Jill's binned on the phone crying her hiballs out and wondering if there is anyfing lefted of their Christmas dinner from yesterday, wot got very quite cancelled and not eated, that they can salvage. And whether there is enuff to share with Lola and Sim. Or to be honest, whether there will be any lefted if Lola and Sim find it first.

Mum says she's going to have all the drinks she couldn't face having yesterday, and all the drinks she planned to have today, right very now. She has never been so relieved in all her life.

Sometimes, she has nightmares about me going missing, and she always feels very quite sorry for anyboddedy who loses their dog, and all this panic with Lola and Sim was much, much too close to actual home.

I has had a lot of cuddles and hunexpected scritches tonight. I fink Mum's head might hurt in the morning ...

December 29

Dear Grandad and Granny Wendy

Fank oo for having me as a actual house guest for Christmas. I did love it, especially when you did realise quite quickly that I are not a bag of carrots or a sack of potatoes wot sleeps in the kitchen at night. Your eyebrows did quite a lot of disappearing into the sky when Mum said I'd be sleeping in their room, but fank oo for not doing Complaints to the Management about that fing. I was mainly a very luffly boy sleeping on my own bed ... mainly. Okay, occasionally. Well, once, if we're completely actual honest about it. But I didn't leave too many muddy footprints on the duvet. I fink they is mainly on the bottom sheet.

Mum and Dad said on the journey down that I was to be on my bestest behaviour, and that Granny Wendy wasn't too sure about dogs. Well, I would like you to know that I are very sure about you. I don't do kissing noses with people wot scare me. I fort it was fabumazing that you did talking to me all the time to tell me wot you was going to do, and we did become very good actual friends big-time-quickly. And Dad is right: you IS a Nangel.

Fank oo for the exerlent fire in the sitting room wot was toasty and comfy and made me very quite sleepy. And for the foxes. You've got billions of them, and I did rolling in most of their poo, but there was so much to be actual honest that it would take me a year to get round to it all.

Everyboddedy mentioned the hills but noboddedy said anyfing about the river. Or the wood. I felted like King Worzel hurling myself down the hill to the woods, and very knackered-flipping-heck-wot-goes-down-must-stagger-back up on the way back to the house. I has donned peeing on as much of the hills and woods and river as I could but I need to do coming back soon to finish the job.

I has donned a lot of sleeping and snoozing since I have come back to Suffolk. All that running downhill and staggering back up has doned fings to the muscles in my bum wot I didn't know they could do. Mum says she feels very actual the same way, too.

I hope I will be allowed to come back very soon.

Lots of love

From your Luffly Boykin

Worzel Wooface

December 31

Someboddedy told me the other day that I are a 'Champion of Dogs.' At first, I did find this quite confuddling and a bit actual hembarrassing, and not quite very true. But then I did some fortful finking and I want to say somefings about this.

I aren't a Champion of Dogs. I can't do clever fings like Mattie-the-Dog-Hexpert's dog. I refuse to do wearing a hat, or always sit when I is told. I don't help peoples answer the phone and I don't find bombs or drugs or sniff out cancer. I aren't a hero.

But that is quite very actual okay. Because wot I are is a normal, famberly dog. I get hupset when the postman scares me, and I dig holes in the garden and ruin-the-blinking-strawberries. Again. And again.

I jump on Dad in the morning and scratch his arm. I biff Mum when I want my breakfast and she wants a lie-in, and I shout at the cats when they try to undo my dinner packets in the kitchen.

I get bored when I don't get my walks cos everyboddedy has Man Flu (okay, when Dad has Man Flu and Mum is knackered from Dad's it's-just-a-cold-WILL-you-stop-snoring), and eat all the letters. I walk muddy footprints all over the floor and then lie on unmade beds to get all the tricky bits of grit out from under my nails.

I am hinconvenient: I take up time, I make peoples change their plans, I delay hollibobs and make visitors stand in the kitchen so I can calm down and decide I aren't scared of them. I cost fundreds of pound of monies when I hurt myself, and I make Mum feel like a total wally sometimes when she gets fings wrong.

I am somefing called a Pri-Orry-Tree. I come first. I get my dinner when Mum has a migraine and I am almost never left on my own. I am only allowed to play with friendly dogs, and I are only allowed to stay with special, careful people who Mum trusts. I are protected and loved, even though I still sometimes do peeing on the carpet when I get over-hexcited.

I hope I do showing wot having a dog – and a rescue dog – is very actual like. I hope peoples henjoy my stories, and see their own dogs, and their own famberlys, and all the mistakes and disasters and good times and sad times, as somefing that happens to everyboddedy who chooses to have a dog in their famberly.

So I aren't a Champion. But I will carry on championing wot being a famberly pet is all about. And perhaps some peoples will decide that having a rescue dog is a good idea for their famberly, even when they do know how much time and monies and love we need. And hopefully, they will very hignore the fuge holes in the garden and not get too actual cross when they find their actual bed full of mud. And wellies.

And maybe when peoples are wondering why their dog won't do sit, they will realise it is a stoopid blinking fing anyway, and probabbly not as himportant as the waggy-tail greeting they do get every single day.

I am Worzel Wooface. I aren't a Champion. I are a luffly boykin, and that's quite very actual good enuff for me.

THE END
(for now)